# CITYSPOTS
# PARIS

**Garry Marchant & Marnie Mitchell**

**Written by Garry Marchant & Marnie Mitchell**
Original photography by Garry Marchant
Front cover photography courtesy of Bernard Bansse/Getty Images
Series design based on an original concept by Studio 183 Limited

**Produced by Cambridge Publishing Management Limited**
Project Editor: Tim Ryder
Layout: Julie Crane
Maps: PC Graphics
Transport map: © Communicarta Ltd

**Published by Thomas Cook Publishing**
A division of Thomas Cook Tour Operations Limited
Company Registration No. 1450464 England
PO Box 227, Unit 18, Coningsby Road
Peterborough PE3 8SB, United Kingdom
email: books@thomascook.com
www.thomascookpublishing.com
+ 44 (0) 1733 416477
ISBN-13: 978-1-84157-640-4
ISBN-10: 1-84157-640-9

**First edition © 2006 Thomas Cook Publishing**
Text © 2006 Thomas Cook Publishing
Maps © 2006 Thomas Cook Publishing
Series/Project Editor: Kelly Anne Pipes
Production/DTP: Steven Collins

Printed and bound in Spain by GraphyCems

# CONTENTS

## INTRODUCING PARIS

Introduction .....................6

When to go.....................8

Bastille Day.....................12

History.....................14

Lifestyle.....................16

Culture .....................18

## MAKING THE MOST OF PARIS

Shopping.....................22

Eating & drinking .....................24

Entertainment & nightlife......28

Sport & relaxation .....................32

Accommodation .....................34

The best of Paris .....................40

Something for nothing ..........44

When it rains.....................46

On arrival.....................48

## THE CITY OF PARIS

Right Bank West.....................62

Right Bank East .....................80

Left Bank .....................98

## OUT OF TOWN

Auvers-sur-Oise .....................122

Reims.....................128

## PRACTICAL INFORMATION

Directory.....................140

Useful phrases.....................154

Emergencies.....................156

## INDEX.....................158

## MAP LIST

Paris city.....................50

Paris transport map.....................54

Right Bank West.....................63

Right Bank East.....................81

Left Bank .....................99

Auvers-sur-Oise .....................123

Reims.....................129

## SYMBOLS & ABBREVIATIONS

The following symbols are used throughout this book:

ⓐ address  ☏ telephone  ⓕ fax  ⓔ email  ⓦ website address
ⓛ opening times  ⓝ public transport connections  ⓘ important

The following symbols are used on the maps:

| | | | |
|---|---|---|---|
| 🛈 information office | | ○ | city |
| ✈ airport | | ○ | large town |
| ➕ hospital | | ∘ | small town |
| 🛡 police station | | ═ | motorway |
| 🚌 bus station | | — | main road |
| 🚆 railway station | | — | minor road |
| Ⓜ metro | | — | railway |
| ✝ cathedral | | | |
| ❶ numbers denote featured cafés & restaurants | | | |

Hotels and restaurants are graded by approximate price as follows:
£ budget  ££ mid-range  £££ expensive

▶ *The Arc de Triomphe standing proud*

# INTRODUCING
Paris

# Introduction

At the end of countless Hollywood romances, when couples finally get together after much tribulation, they invariably fly off to Paris.

Paris is the lovers' dream city, a vision of romance and eternal honeymoon. Grand visionaries built this capital of broad, tree-lined boulevards such as the Champs-Elysées and Saint-Germain, and of magnificent monuments such as the Arc de Triomphe, the Louvre, the Eiffel Tower, Notre-Dame cathedral and the gold-domed Invalides. Even city hall, the Hôtel de Ville, is a work of art.

Yet Paris remains an ancient city of quaint cobbled streets, hidden squares, fountains, statues, and the Seine with its 37 unique bridges. Aimlessly strolling through Paris is a real delight and a voyage of constant discovery.

The attraction is much more than stone, brick and marble, however artistically assembled. There is something in the air of Paris that inspires romance. In this city where the good life is an art, couples kiss tenderly in the streets, people linger in sidewalk cafés and leisure time is treasured.

The traditional city of cancan dancers and the Louvre, of accordion players in the metro and booksellers along the Seine, endures. Yet Paris isn't stodgy or old-fashioned. The young, dynamic mayor, Bertrand Delanoë, is changing the city, giving it back to the people. Every Sunday, traffic is blocked on the Right Bank quays and pedestrians take over.

On Friday nights and Sunday afternoons, rivers of roller-bladers flow through the streets. Several years ago, the city turned a section of the city-centre quays into an instant beach, Paris Plage, in the summer. It has been such a success that cities across Europe have copied it. In winter, the first level of the Eiffel Tower becomes a skating rink, so skaters can glide around, 57 m (187 ft) above the city.

Paris, a centre of culture and fashion, food and fun, is one of the world's most attractive, lively cities. For its many attractions, Paris is the world's most visited city, with 26 million visitors a year. And 26 million tourists can't be wrong.

When young lovers return home from their dream visit, they will know, to paraphrase the memorable line from the old Bogart/Bergman movie *Casablanca*, that they'll always have Paris.

⏶ *How high do you dare climb?*

## When to go

### SEASONS & CLIMATE

'I love Paris in the springtime', goes the old refrain, and while the city is at its most beautiful in this season, it is worth visiting year-round. Summer can be hot, but it is generally pleasant, with long daylight hours, the many green spaces and the ubiquitous street cafés. In August, many Parisians leave the city for their annual vacation (although this tradition is changing as work patterns become more flexible), so many non-central restaurants, cafés and small businesses close.

Tourists descend on the city year-round, but particularly in July and August, so queues at museums and other attractions can be long. During autumn, parks, gardens and tree-lined boulevards are awash with rich colours and cheery gold, red and yellow leaves pattern the ground. Children are heading back to school (*rentrée*) and days get shorter and cooler.

Paris can be grey and gloomy in autumn and winter, but its cultural life is bright. This is an especially good time to see its excellent museums, monuments, galleries and many other indoor attractions.

### ANNUAL EVENTS

There is always something going on in Paris, more than even a resident could ever hope to attend. For the latest information on events, see www.parisinfo.com

#### January–February

Paris-wide sales last from mid-January to late February. Larger shops take all the major credit cards.

**April**

**Grandes Eaux Musicales (musical fountain displays)** Performed on Saturdays, Sundays and some public holidays from April to the start of October. ❸ Parc du Château de Versailles ❶ bookings 01 30 83 78 89 ❿ www.chateauversailles-spectacles.fr

**Marathon de Paris** A 42-km (25-mile) footrace through Paris, starting at the Champs-Elysées. ❿ www.parismarathon.com

**May–June**

**French Open Tennis Championships** ❸ Stade Roland-Garros, 2 avenue Gordon-Bennett ❶ 01 47 43 48 00 ❿ www.rolandgarros.com ⓜ Metro: Porte d'Auteuil

**Musique Côté Jardin** Music is performed in the city's parks and gardens from May to October.

**June–July**

**47th International Paris Air Show** (18–24 June, 2007). The show will be open to the public on Friday 22 June, Saturday 23 June and Sunday 24 June. ❸ Le Bourget airport ❿ www.salon-du-bourget.fr or http://bourget.epistema.com

**Paris Jazz Festival** The best of jazz played from early June to the end of July. ❸ Parc Floral de Paris ❶ 01 42 76 47 12 ❿ www.parcfloraldeparis.com

**Festival Chopin** A celebration of the composer from 17 June to 14 July.

**July**

**Bastille Day** (14 July). Celebrate France's national holiday with dances on the 13th, and a parade down the Champs-Elysées with jets and fireworks swooping overhead. ❶ 01 42 76 47 12

**Finale of the Tour de France** (End of July). ⓐ Avenue des Champs-Elysées ⓦ www.letour.fr

**Finale of the Peking to Paris Motor Challenge** A classic car rally celebrating the 100th anniversary of the first transcontinental motor marathon ends in Paris in July 2007. ⓣ (44) 12 35 85 12 91 ⓦ www.siteset.co.uk/pekingparis/

### July–August

**Paris Plage** From mid-July to mid-August, the Right Bank quays of the Seine in the city centre are transformed into a faux beach, with music, food, sand and palm trees, boules and a general festive, party atmosphere. Following the success of this trend-setting event, cities from Berlin to Rome have created their own versions. ⓣ 01 42 76 47 12 ⓦ www.paris.fr

**Festival Cinéma au Clair de Lune (Open-air Cinema)** Complete with a giant outdoor screen, film favourites and a party atmosphere. ⓐ Parc de la Villette ⓦ www.villette.com

**Quartier d'Eté Festival (Summer Festival)** Music, movies and other happenings throughout Paris from mid-July to late August.

### August–September

**Jazz at La Villette** Top names and new artists converge at the Parc de la Villette for this music shindig from the end of August to mid-September. ⓦ www.villette.com

**Les Fêtes de Nuit** Splendid sound and light show from late August to mid-September at the château's Bassin de Neptune. ⓐ Parc du Château de Versailles ⓦ www.chateauversailles-spectacles.fr

## September

**Journées du Patrimoine** Normally off-limits buildings such as the Palais de l'Elysée, the president's residence, are opened to the public for one weekend in September. ⓦ www.jp.culture.fr

**Paris Autumn Festival** Celebrates autumnal events from mid-September to the end of December. ⓦ www.festival-automne.com

**Coupe du Monde de Rugby 2007** World Cup Rugby plays out at the Stade de France from 7 September to 20 October, 2007.

## October

**Nuit Blanche (Sleepless Night)** All night (usually 1 October) you can visit the normally hidden side of Paris, revealed through performances, monument visits and installations. ☎ 01 42 76 47 12 ⓦ www.paris.fr

### PUBLIC HOLIDAYS

Most shops and all government offices including banks and post offices are closed on public holidays, as are some museums.

**New Year's Day** 1 January
**Easter** late March/early April
**May Day** 1 May
**Victory Day, WW II** 8 May
**Ascension Thursday** May
**Bastille Day** 14 July
**Assumption of the Virgin Mary** 15 August
**All Saints Day** 1 November
**1918 Armistice Day** 11 November
**Christmas Day** 25 December

# Bastille Day

The French celebrate Bastille Day (*fête nationale* to the locals) with great enthusiasm, especially in Paris. The main national holiday marks the anniversary of the storming of the Bastille on 14 July, 1789. It was the symbolic starting point of the French Revolution, and the end of the French monarchy.

Bastille Day starts with a grand military parade down the Champs-Elysées, with tanks, fighter jets and colourfully costumed servicemen. It continues with celebrations all over the city, including grand balls, ending with massive fireworks displays and crowds thronging in the streets.

While nothing remains of the historic old stone prison (a café now stands on the original site), the Bastille area has become one of the city's liveliest. Place de la Bastille and the small streets off it (especially rue de Lappe) buzz with action year-round.

The opening of the Opéra Bastille on 13 July, 1989, revitalised the once-grubby working-class neighbourhood in eastern Paris. Old buildings were restored and thousands of homes built. The new opera house did more than bring high culture to the Bastille. The area quickly became a trendy quarter for gallery owners and young artists.

In 1995 an abandoned railway viaduct that once carried trains from the Bastille to the eastern suburbs and a park outside the city was reopened. The attractive red-brick arcade of the Viaduc des Arts now houses chic boutiques offering offbeat fashion, arts and crafts. Large windows along the viaduct look into some 50 artisans' galleries, studios, workshops and design shops. Fashionable coffee shops and restaurants offer outdoor seating under blinds or awnings. The top of the viaduct is a 4.5-km-long (2.8-miles) elevated green park, the Promenade Plantée, running all the way to the Bois de Vincennes.

Every Thursday and Sunday from 08.30 to 13.00 the vast Marché Bastille opens on boulevard Richard-Lenoir. The market offers mostly food, but also a variety of crafts and clothing, leather goods, lingerie and textiles. On Sundays, performers sing and play, bringing a festive atmosphere to this once run-down area.

Chic art galleries, shops and theatres have also located to the Bastille. At night, earthy dance clubs, restaurants, bars and all-night music joints enliven one of the trendiest sections of Paris. And every evening, young Parisians – and visitors – once more storm the Bastille, not with mayhem in mind, but merely a good time.

△ *Scenes from the uprisings are depicted in Bastille metro station*

# History

The glamorous French capital at the crossroads of Europe started as a fishing and trading village on a small island, now the Île-de-la-Cité, on the Seine river. Between 250 and 200 BC, a Gallic tribe, the Parisii, settled here because the islands made it easy to cross the river, and the river formed a natural moat. In troubled times, the Parisiis abandoned their Left Bank produce farms, crossed to the islands and burned their wooden bridges behind them.

When Julius Caesar's Roman legions invaded in 52 BC, the Parisii torched their island fort and abandoned it. The Romans extended the town to the Left Bank, built baths and a forum, and laid a grid of streets. The expanded town became known as Lutetia (Latin for 'mid-water dwelling'), then Civitas Parisiorum or Paris. But it remained a relatively minor outpost of the Roman Empire.

Politics, rather than geography, determined the city's fate. France was governed from Lyon until the 9th century, when Capetian kings made Paris the capital and started rebuilding.

The massive egos of kings and emperors gave Paris its beauty. Over the centuries, they commissioned engineers and artisans who created poetry in stone, marble and steel, as a legacy to themselves. Most of these grand edifices are located on or near the river; the stretch from Pont d'Austerlitz to Pont Alexandre III is now a UNESCO World Heritage Site.

During the French Revolution, Paris was the centre stage of French history, with the storming of the Bastille prison in 1789 and the overthrow of the monarchy in 1792.

Paris developed steadily during the Industrial Revolution, the French Second Empire, and the Belle Epoque. The city's distinctive architectural style was finally set in stone when Napoleon III

(1852–70) commissioned Baron Georges Eugène Haussmann to radically transform it from a medieval city to a glorious 19th-century capital. The baron created modern Paris, with broad boulevards and the distinctive, six- to eight-floor Haussmann-style buildings in *pierre de taille* (cut stone) that line the Seine. Haussmann also added new water systems to keep the river clean, rebuilt the Île-de-la-Cité and added four new bridges.

In the tumultuous 19th and 20th centuries, Paris suffered from the ravages of war. During the Franco-Prussian War Siege of Paris (1870–71), the locals, ever the gourmets, ate the zoo animals. During World War II, German troops occupied the city from 1940 to 1944.

The latter half of the 20th century featured a number of major building projects, including the Centre Pompidou. The construction of La Défense, in the northwestern outskirts, created a secondary city centre of steel and glass, where modern high-rises now house local and multinational businesses. The Tour Montparnasse and the Bibliothèque Nationale, the national library in the 13th *arrondissement*, were less successful additions to the city.

Today, Paris is the headquarters of many international trade and social organisations, including the Organisation for Economic Cooperation & Development and UNESCO, in addition to the head offices of nearly half of all French companies, and the offices of many major international firms.

Paris, the world's most-visited city, remains a cultural, economic, political, financial and transport centre of Europe.

### AIR MAIL

During the Siege of Paris between 23 September 1870 and 22 January 1871, officials used balloon mail. Some 65 unguided mail balloons were discharged, of which only two disappeared.

## Lifestyle

For all its world-renowned monuments, Paris is not a museum but a living city, although Parisians are certainly passionate museum-goers and will often line up for blocks in order to catch a new exposition. The Place du Palais Royal, across from the Louvre, is often buzzing with activity, whether it's skateboarders weaving round coloured cones, rap or rock musicians jamming, or a country food

⬤ *Take a break at a streetside café*

falr selling *pain de compagne* (rustic bread) or *saucisson* (sausage). In many neighbourhoods, food markets are held on weekends, when Parisians patronise their local neighbourhood stalls.

Parisians love to gather at cafés, squares and along the quays and pedestrian bridges (such as the Pont des Arts), whenever time and weather permit. To return central Paris to the people, the City Council closes the Seine-side expressways to traffic and opens them to pedestrians on Sundays and public holidays. The result is a huge success, with strollers, cyclists, skaters and loungers taking over the riverbanks. On Sundays along the newly popular Canal St-Martin in the 10th *arrondissement*, the quai de Valmy and quai de Jemmapes are also turned over to pedestrians.

The Place de l'Hôtel de Ville, in front of the town hall, buzzes with activity year-round. In summer, sand and palm trees are transported here for public volleyball courts during the hugely successful Paris Plage (see page 10) when the quays of the centre are turned into a riverside 'beach'. In the winter, the square transforms into an ice rink, with free rentals and festive music. The latest ice rink of note, and a huge hit with the locals in winter, is 57 m (188 ft) above ground on the first level of the Eiffel Tower.

On fine days, Parisians can be seen walking their dogs or occupying every inch of space on lawns and metal chairs in such parks as the Jardin du Luxembourg and the Jardin des Tuileries. Whatever the weather, locals love getting together with family and friends, and young people and couples linger for hours at street cafés, cell phones in one hand, cigarettes in another. The government is trying to outlaw smoking in some public areas such as restaurants and bars, but the liberty-loving French stubbornly cling to their habits. Sunday, a day for families, is quiet in the city and is often spent dining out or at home *en famille*.

# Culture

Paris has always been a centre of architectural innovation. Both the Eiffel Tower and, more recently, I M Pei's glass Pyramid at the Louvre, sparked controversy when they were first built. Today, they are heralded as marvels of innovative design.

Though it was designed some 30 years ago, the Centre Pompidou, which houses the Museum of Modern Art, is considered revolutionary. Despite the view of some Parisians that the chunky exterior pipes are worthy of a plumber's nightmare, the building is a success for its museum space and panoramic view across Paris.

Another example of original design is taking shape along the Seine, beneath the Eiffel Tower. The new Musée du Quai Branly, designed by Jean Nouvel and scheduled to open in 2006, has a principal façade that follows the curve of the river, as well as a 'living culture' space for theatre, music and dance.

As one of the world's cultural capitals, Paris always has exhibits of such great artists as Ingres, Chagall and Monet, but springing up in the north Marais neighbourhood is also to be found a wonderful collection of small, unpretentious, designer boutiques and art galleries. Among the new, young fashion designers are Gaspard Yurkievich, with a boutique and showroom on rue Charlot, and the *multimarque* boutique (selling numerous designer labels), Shine, nearby. Fresh new galleries housing contemporary art in the Marais are Chantal Croussel, Denise René and Frédéric Giroux (all on rue Charlot).

Even for locals, the choice in Paris can be overwhelming, with some 1,800 classified monuments, 140 museums and 145 theatres.

---

● *Behold this bizarre statue!*

The weekly publication *Pariscope*, with complete event listings, has around 50 pages dedicated to theatres alone, from café-style to cabarets and dinner shows. The museums range from the great, such as the Louvre and the Musée d'Orsay, to the offbeat, such as the Musée de l'Erotisme and the Musée de la Contrefacon, the latter boasting a fascinating collection of counterfeit objects, from food to perfumes. Freshly opened is the Musée d'Art Moderne de la Ville de Paris on avenue du President Wilson in the 16th *arrondissement*, and the Musée de l'Orangerie in the Tuileries in the 1st.

The two opera houses, the majestic Palais Garnier with its gold leaf embellishments and the modern glass-fronted Opéra Bastille, opened for the bicentennial of the French Revolution, provide a full and varied programme of opera and ballet throughout the year (except August). In an effort to get younger audiences to attend operatic and ballet performances, the Opéra Bastille installed 62 standing places, for just €5 per performance, purchased with cash or credit card at ticket-issuing machines. This has been so successful that the same system will soon be installed at the Garnier.

Performing arts venues range from the mega, such as the Palais des Congrès, to the mini of the cloakroom-sized cabarets and theatres in Montmartre.

Even the quality of the busker is higher in Paris than in many cities, and student musicians can often be heard giving impressive renditions of such works as Vivaldi's *Four Seasons* in the metro, while a talented pianist plunks out a toe-tapping ragtime tune on his old piano on the boulevard Saint-Michel in Luxembourg.

◗ *A spectacular view of the city*

# MAKING THE MOST OF
Paris

# Shopping

Paris is the epicentre of haute couture, with all the top names occupying select addresses along the avenue Montaigne, Champs-Elysées, Faubourg Saint-Honoré and rue Saint-Honoré, Place Vendôme and rue Royale. Even if you can only afford to window shop, it is fun to stroll past such bastions of high fashion as Cartier, Chanel, Louis Vuitton, Gucci, Dior, Lalique, Longchamps, Hermes, Christian Lacroix, Jean-Paul Gaultier and Versace. There is even a list of officially sanctioned haute couture houses at www.modeaparis.com

You can get a cross-section of goods in the city's excellent department stores, such as Galeries Lafayette and Le Printemps on boulevard Haussmann in the 9th *arrondissement*, Bon Marché, with its famous food store, in the 7th, and the BHV, across from the Hôtel de Ville in the 1st. All have the latest in ready-to-wear fashions as well as household items.

Metrosexuals have their own outlets in such venues as Madelios, near the Place de la Madeleine, which features such men's brands as Hugo Boss and Cerruti Jeans. Likewise, Le Printemps has a separate building devoted to menswear.

The Marais, the city's oldest district, where ancient buildings lean into cobbled streets, has an eclectic variety of little boutiques. Although Sunday shopping is largely prohibited (a regulation that is under review), it somehow carries on unnoticed in the Marais (mainly in the 4th), where, on oft-sombre Sundays, busy shops add welcome animation to such streets as Francs Bourgeois and to the newly fashionable Canal St-Martin district in the 10th *arrondissement*. Here, *branché* (trendy) boutiques around the quays (Valmy and Jemmapes) and side streets also evade Sunday closings.

> **SHOPPING TIP**
> Annual sales, from around mid-January to late February and in
> the summer (June/July), offer huge discounts and bargains.

Across the river in the celebrated Left Bank, boulevard Saint-
Germain is the thoroughfare to shop, sip coffee, stroll and people-
watch. As well as the boulevard itself, its side streets, rue Four and
rue des Saint-Pères, and the streets around St Sulpice church are full
of little boutiques selling such items as daring lingerie and funky
embroidered bags.

Also not to be missed are the city's many markets, specialising in
everything from farm-produced cheeses to *grand-mère's* antiques.

For a stylish memento of your stay, the museum boutiques,
selling art cards, prints and classy trinkets, are worth a browse.

---

### USEFUL SHOPPING PHRASES

**What time do the shops open/close?**
A quelle heure ouvrent/ferment les magasins?
*Ah kehlur oovr/fehrm leh mahgazhang?*

**How much is this?**
C'est combien?
*Cey combyahng?*

**Can I try this on?**
Puis-je essayer ceci?
*Pweezh ehssayeh cerssee?*

**My size is...**
Ma taille (clothes)/
ma pointure (shoes) est ...
*Mah tie/mah pooahngtewr ay ...*

**I'll take this one, thank you**
Je prends celui-ci/celle-ci merci
*Zher prahng serlweesi/
sehlsee mehrsee*

# Eating & drinking

As a world culinary capital, Paris has an impressive variety of restaurants, brasseries and bistros. With 10,000 bars and restaurants, the only problem is making a choice. Dedicated gourmets can dine at the *crème de la crème*, the chefs' restaurants such as Fogon and L'ami Jean. You can dine with a view at the Michelin-rated 2-star Tour d'Argent and the Philippe Starck-designed Kong, where views are superb and lofty, and prices are pretty rarefied, too.

One recent trend is renowned chefs opening small *prix d'amis* (affordable price) restaurants to bring fine food to a wider group of discerning diners. Alain Senderens renounced his three Michelin stars to set up the unpretentious Senderens restaurant in place de la Madeleine. Pierre Gagnaire opened the popular Gaya in the 7th *arrondissement* and others are following suit.

For those on a budget, many restaurants serve set meals of several courses, with entrée and *plat* (main course), or *plat* and dessert, or all three for a fixed fee. Bistros offer home-style cooking in an informal atmosphere, while brasseries provide sandwiches, salads or simple meals most of the day. Wine bars have quality wines and often have tasty snacks or meals to accompany them.

Too many simple restaurants and brasseries, especially in tourist areas, limit their menus to roast chicken or steak with chips. If you'd

## PRICE RATINGS
Restaurant ratings in this book are based on the average price of a three-course dinner without drinks:
£ up to €30; ££ €30–€50; £££ above €50

like something other than chips, they may provide a salad or vegetable instead. Despite their modest surroundings and prices, many brasseries and bistros serve market-fresh produce.

Eating places are found throughout the city, and often those away from the main tourist sites are of better value and quality. The greatest collection of budget restaurants is in the popular and touristy Saint-Michel area in the Latin Quarter. The warren of cobbled streets near place Saint-Michel, especially along rues Huchette, Harpe and St-Severin, is crammed with little restaurants and bars. Some places have regional French fare, many are Greek, while Asian, Tunisian and even Mexican cuisines are also represented. Most prices are low and quality is often lacking, but some of these restaurants serve quite reasonable meals.

The Montmartre area is known for its African restaurants, serving such dishes as *mafé* (West African meat in peanut sauce) and *yassa* (Senegalese chicken, mutton or fish in a lemon, mustard and onion sauce). Chinese fare is authentic and plentiful in the 13th *arrondissement*, Japanese along rue St-Anne in the 2nd, and Indian restaurants can be found in passage Brady in the 10th. *Traiteurs* (takeaways), especially

🔺 *A restaurant on the Left Bank*

Chinese, serve budget meals and sometimes you can eat on the premises. They are simple, but good value. (For more info on ethnic food, see 'Ethnic Paris', pages 118–20.)

French fare changes with the seasons. In autumn and winter, fishmongers set up stalls in front of many brasseries and serve fresh oysters. During cold months, hearty, warming cheese dishes from the mountain region of the Savoy – fondues, *raclettes* and *tartiflettes* – are popular. In summer, fresh fruits and vegetables are plentiful in markets and on menus and Parisians love dining *al fresco* late into the evening.

It is advisable to book ahead for any of the grand establishments, although it is not necessary for simple restaurants or brasseries, which, unless they are the trendiest places, can be booked on the day you wish to visit. More time should be allowed for reserving at haute cuisine restaurants, which often need to be booked weeks in advance and confirmed the day before. At the more exclusive restaurants, men should wear a jacket and tie, especially in the evenings. Otherwise, the dress code is fairly relaxed. Many restaurants are closed on Sunday, but the local weekly listings publication, *Pariscope*, lists some venues that are open (*ouvert le dimanche*).

Few of France's top restaurants and traditional brasseries are vegetarian-friendly, though some simple cafés, takeaways and

### DINING TIPS

Many restaurants serve lunches that are half of the price of the same meal served for dinner, so often locals dine out at lunch and the tourists at dinner.

A 15 per cent service charge is included in the bill, but you can round up the bill at your discretion.

## USEFUL DINING PHRASES

**I would like a table for ... people**
Je voudrais une table pour ... personnes
*Zher voodray ewn tabl poor ... pehrson*

**Waiter/waitress!**
Monsieur/Mademoiselle,
s'il vous plaît!
M'sewr/madmwahzel,
sylvooplay!

**May I have the bill, please?**
L'addition, s'il vous plaît!
*Laddyssyawng, sylvooplay!*

**Could I have it well-cooked/medium/rare please?**
Je le voudrais bien cuit/à point/saignant
*Zher ler voodray beeang kwee/ah pwang/saynyang*

**I am a vegetarian. Does this contain meat?**
Je suis végétarien (végétarienne). Est-ce que ce plat contient
de la viande?
*Zher swee vehzhehtarianhg (vehzhehtarien). Essker ser plah
kontyang der lah veeahngd?*

**Where is the toilet (restroom) please?**
Où sont les toilettes, s'il vous plaît?
*Oo sawng leh twahlaitt, sylvooplay?*

lunch counters are starting to serve *bio* (organic) fare. One, started
by two chefs and known for its quality, is Eatme (ⓦ www.eatme.fr).
A nutritionist even approves the dishes that are served here.

# Entertainment & nightlife

From all-night discos to cosy wine bars and what some euphemistically call 'naughty Paris', the city truly has something for every nightlife temperament. Whether your aim is to relax, have fun or *se cultiver* (get cultured), there is no lack of choice in Paris.

The long summer nights in Paris give Parisians several more hours of daylight after their work day, when they can dine or drink at outdoor restaurants and bars. Free summer concerts fill the parks and gardens from around May to September, while festivals and music fêtes fill the streets and bars with a lively, late-night atmosphere during sultry months.

Trendy (what some Parisians call *hype attitude*) clubs include Le Rex (www.rexclub.com), Le Pulp (www.pulp-paris.com) and Le Triptyque (www.letriptyque.com) in the 2nd *arrondissement*, or Le Nouveau Casino (www.nouveaucasino.net) in the recently hip nightlife district of rue Oberkampf in the 11th. The Bastille district in the 11th is an ever-popular people place with a party atmosphere among its bistros, clubs and bars.

The river after dark is as bright with action as it is with lights, aided by such floating clubs as Le Batofar and La Guinguette Pirate in the 13th *arrondissement* and the Bâteau Six Huit on quai Montebello in the 5th. Such riverine scenes offer the best in electro, house and rhythm-and-blues. Another waterside district that has become fashionable is the Canal St-Martin in the 10th *arrondissement*, its quays (Valmy and Jemmapes) and side streets buzzing with interesting restaurants and bars.

Jazz-lovers head for the numerous clubs on rue des Lombards near Les Halles and the famous Caveau de la Huchette on the street of the same name in the Saint-Michel district.

Paris has some 100 dance clubs, so for those who want to go clubbing, there's something for everyone, from rock, rap, hip-hop and techno to African rhythms, salsa and samba. Those who literally

◆ *A typical Parisian bar in the evening*

MOULIN ROUGE
A LOCO
CERRUTI 1881
présente le
1er Trophée MOULIN ROUGE
DU
ULIN RO
FORMIDA

like to party all night long should ask bartenders or party-hearty Parisians where the 'after' bars, often unadvertised, are. Many are in the lively Pigalle area of Montmartre.

In a country synonymous with fine wine, wine bars or quiet places to *boire un verre* (have a drink) are plentiful and varied. Among the cosy and atmospheric are Le Café Marly in the Louvre, the China Club in the 12th *arrondissement*, and the Henri IV along the Pont Neuf.

The major museums have at least one late-night opening (see listings in 'The City' section) for culture vultures, while the Opéra National de Paris stages the best of opera and ballet performances at its sumptuous Palais Garnier and its modern Opéra Bastille, known for its daring productions.

If just vegging out and seeing the latest Hollywood or French film is your thing, Paris has all the major films in *version originale* (VO) in cinemas at such central locations as the 6th *arrondissement*, the Champs-Elysées, Les Halles and Montparnasse.

Scantily-clad cancan girls in cabaret-type performances strut their stuff in Le Lido, Le Moulin Rouge and Le Crazy Horse, among others. The weekly *Pariscope* or *L'Officiel des Spectacles*, available at newsstands, list the full spectrum of more serious eroticism. These two publications also provide up-to-date listings (only in French) of movies, live theatre, expositions, sporting events, guided visits and even restaurants.

The oft-quoted old phrase 'gay Paree' has taken on a new meaning in this city, with the gay and bi community converging on the 'gay Marais' and the Queen nightclub (which heteros love too) on the Champs-Elysées.

◀ Moulin Rouge *is a great entertainment venue*

# Sport & relaxation

## PARTICIPATION SPORTS

### Bicycling

Bicycling is a popular, convenient recreation in this city with more than 100 km (62 miles) of cycle lanes. Tourist information offices and bicycle rental shops provide free leaflets detailing cycle routes.

### Ice-skating

In winter, the square in front of the Hôtel de Ville becomes a popular skating rink. You can rent skates at the rink-side. The newest ice rink, and one with a view, is on the first level of the Eiffel Tower. Skating and skate rentals are free to tower ticket-holders.

### Jogging

Joggers can follow the Seine either down by the riverside or along the streets above. They can also run in and around larger parks such as Luxembourg. The Jardin des Tuileries has a jogging trail, and Paris's main parks have numerous running and walking tracks.

### Roller-blading

Paris is a world capital of roller-blading. More than 4,000 skaters leave from the Place d'Italie at 22.00 every Friday night for a 25-km (15-mile) circuit. Details of the route are posted the day before on www.pari-roller.com. The skateathons are open to all, but skaters should be reasonably proficient to join in. Beginner roller-bladers should choose the Sunday afternoon events that leave from outside Nomades (see opposite). The 20-km (12½-mile), three-hour circuit starts at 14.00. See www.rollers-coquillages.org for more details. Skates are available for rent at:

**Ilios** ⓐ 4 allée Vivaldi ⓣ 01 44 74 75 76 ⓝ Metro: Daumesnil
**Nomades** ⓐ 37 boulevard Bourdon ⓣ 01 44 54 07 44 ⓝ Metro: Bastille

## SPECTATOR SPORTS
### Football & rugby
Fans can see professional football and rugby matches either at the
Stade de France or the smaller Parc des Princes, the home stadium
of the Paris soccer team, Paris Saint-Germain.
**Parc des Princes** ⓐ 24 rue du Commandant Guilbaud ⓣ 01 47 43 71 71,
tickets 0825 075 078 ⓝ Metro: Porte de Saint-Cloud
**Stade de France** ⓐ 93216 Saint-Denis la Plaine ⓣ 0892 700 900
ⓦ www.stadefrance.fr ⓝ Metro: Stade de France

### Horse racing
Enthusiasts can find flat racing at the Hippodrome Longchamp and
steeplechase and trotting at the Hippodrome d'Auteuil, both in the
Bois de Boulogne. There is also steeplechase and trotting at the
Hippodrome de Vincennes in the Bois de Vincennes. For information
on all venues, see www.france-galop.com
**Hippodrome d'Auteuil** ⓐ route des Lacs ⓣ 01 40 71 47 47 ⓝ Metro:
Porte d'Auteuil
**Hippodrome Longchamp** ⓐ route de Tribunes, Bois de Boulogne
ⓣ 01 44 30 75 00 ⓝ Metro: Porte d'Auteuil
**Hippodrome de Vincennes** ⓐ 2 route de la Ferme ⓣ 01 49 77 17 17
ⓝ Metro: Château de Vincennes

### Tennis
The Roland-Garros stadium is the home of the French Open.
**Stade Roland-Garros** ⓐ 2 avenue Gordon-Bennett ⓣ 01 47 43 48 00
ⓦ www.rolandgarros.com ⓝ Métro: Porte d'Auteuil

# Accommodation

Although international lodging chains are here, most Paris hotels are small, independent establishments. Rooms are often small and elevators can be rickety or nonexistent, but generally these hotels have distinct, charming atmospheres. Service can range from surly to warm and accommodating.

Paris also has a great variety of good mid-range, boutique hostelries, with the most attractive called *hotels de charme*. Many are set in stately old residences, former monasteries, even churches. What these lodgings lack in space, they make up for in character and personal service. Many have been renovated in recent years, so have modern bathrooms and facilities such as satellite TV and internet and fax connections.

Two-star hotels and above must be competent in at least one foreign language, usually English. Reserve as soon as possible, by email, fax or telephone. Internet booking is becoming increasingly popular, with even the small hotels. All hotels post their rates at the entrance and visitors can walk in off the street to book a room, but this is not advisable during holiday seasons.

In the budget category, with an average rate of €83, Paris is the third least-expensive city in Europe, after Budapest and Frankfurt, according to a survey commissioned by the tourist board.

The Paris Visitors Bureau's excellent website is a good central booking site: www.parisinfo.com. Also try www.hotels-paris.com

## PRICE RATINGS
Accommodation ratings are based on the average price of a double room per night, including breakfast:
£ up to €100; ££ €100–€200; £££ over €200

Below is just a small sampling of the 1,449 hotels in Paris, with special emphasis on those with unique characters or histories. If you're calling from outside France, dial 33 (country code) and drop the 'o' before dialling the number.

## RIGHT BANK WEST

**New Orient Hotel £** This small (30 rooms), charming hotel is in a quiet neighbourhood, but is near a market, restaurants and cafés. Some rooms have balconies. ❷ 16 rue de Constantinople, 75008 ❶ 01 45 22 21 64 ❶ 01 42 93 83 23 Ⓦ www.hotel-paris-orient.com Ⓜ Metro: Europe, Villiers or St-Lazare

🔺 *The charming Caron de Beaumarchais hotel*

**Hôtel Duminy Vendôme ££** Just a few blocks from the Louvre and the Jardin des Tuileries, this comfortable hotel is classic, yet modern, with coffee maker and WiFi in the rooms. ⓐ 3/5 rue du Mont Thabor, 75001 ⓣ 01 55 33 16 55 ⓕ 01 55 33 16 56 ⓦ www.HotelDuminyVendome.com ⓝ Metro: Tuileries

**Hôtel La Sanguine ££** The Sanguine has a convenient location (near the Place de la Madeleine), friendly staff and good breakfasts for around €7. ⓐ 6 rue de Surène, 75008 ⓣ 01 42 65 71 61 ⓕ 01 42 66 96 77 ⓝ Metro: Madeleine

**Hôtel Relais Saint-Honoré ££** Ideal for those planning to spend their time in the Louvre and the Jardin des Tuileries, the hotel, in a 17th-century building, has bedrooms with period furniture, ceiling beams and tasteful décor. The hotel provides free broadband internet access. ⓐ 308 rue Saint-Honoré, 75001 ⓣ 01 42 96 06 06 ⓕ 01 42 96 17 50 ⓦ www.relaissainthonore.com ⓝ Metro: Tuileries

**Hôtel Atala £££** The 48-room Atala near the Champs-Elysées has a bright, cheery garden for fair-weather breakfasting and dining. Built in 1929, the hotel is roomy by Parisian standards, and the 6th, 7th and 8th floors have good views. ⓐ 10 rue Chateaubriand, 75008 ⓣ 01 45 62 01 62 ⓕ 01 42 25 66 38 ⓦ www.hotel-atala.com ⓝ Metro: Charles de Gaulle-Etoile

### RIGHT BANK EAST
**Caron de Beaumarchais £** Beautifully decorated (perhaps over-elaborate for some tastes), friendly and well located. ⓐ 12 rue Vieille du Temple, 75004 ⓣ 01 42 72 34 12 ⓐ 01 42 72 34 63 ⓦ www.carondebeaumarchais.com ⓝ Metro: Hôtel de Ville

**Hôtel du 7ème Art £** This unusual little hotel has a Hollywood theme, with numerous posters, photos and other memorabilia from the golden era of movies. Rooms are small, and there is no elevator. ⓐ 20 rue Saint-Paul, 75004 ⓣ 01 44 54 85 00 ⓕ 01 42 77 69 10

**Hôtel Saint Merry £** This unique hotel in the heart of the historical Marais quarter, originally a presbytery, then a brothel, is a restored 18th-century stone building with lots of character. ⓐ 78 rue de la Verrerie, 75004 ⓣ 01 42 78 14 15 ⓕ 01 40 29 06 82 ⓦ www.hotelmarais.com

**Hôtel de Lutèce ££** Set in a 17th-century building, it has a pleasant lobby, rugs on tiled floors, a fireplace, and huge, ancient wooden roof beams across the high, white-washed ceiling. The 23 small rooms are tastefully decorated. ⓐ 65 rue Saint-Louis-en-l'Île, 75004 ⓣ 01 43 26 23 52 ⓕ 01 43 29 60 25 ⓦ www.paris-hotel-lutece.com ⓝ Metro: Pont Marie

### LEFT BANK
**Hôtel Cluny Sorbonne £** Set in an 18th-century building in the centre of the Latin Quarter, the hotel is within walking distance of attractions such as Notre-Dame, the Panthéon and the Louvre. Rimbaud, the great French *enfant terrible* poet, stayed here in 1872. ⓐ 8 rue Victor Cousin, 75005 ⓣ 01 43 54 66 66 ⓕ 01 43 29 68 07 ⓦ www.hotel-cluny.fr ⓝ Metro: Cluny-La Sorbonne or Luxembourg

**Hôtel des Jardins du Luxembourg ££** The best rooms in this Haussmann-style hotel have small balconies overlooking the quiet street. Some psychiatrists stay here, perhaps because Sigmund Freud was a guest in 1885. ⓐ 5 Impasse Royer-Collard, 75005

🕿 01 40 46 08 88 📠 01 40 46 02 28 🌐 www.les-jardins-du-luxembourg.com Ⓜ Metro: Cluny-La Sorbonne

**Hôtel des Marronniers ££** A private courtyard entrance leads to this charming hotel, and a private garden off the breakfast room is a haven in the centre of the city. 📍 21 rue Jacob, 75006 🕿 01 43 25 30 60 📠 01 40 46 83 56 🌐 www.hotel-marronniers.com Ⓜ Metro: Odéon or Saint-Germain-des-Prés

🔺 *A hotel room in Caron de Beaumarchais*

**Hôtel dc Buci £££** Near fashionable boulevard Saint-Germain, the Buci is soothingly atmospheric, with leather chairs in the lobby, potted palms and an intriguing collection of Art Deco paintings and statues. The staff is especially helpful. ⓐ 22 rue Buci, 75006 ⓣ 01 55 42 74 74 ⓕ 01 55 42 74 44 ⓦ www.bucihotel.com ⓜ Metro: Saint-Germain-des-Prés or Mabillon

## YOUTH HOSTELS

A network of youth hostels (Auberges de Jeunesse) offers comfortable, inexpensive accommodation for members. There are also numerous youth accommodation centres based in former hotels, which don't require membership. The Paris website, www.parisinfo.com, lists hostels, campsites and long-stay apartments. The following are good choices:

**Auberge Internationale des Jeunes** The age limit here is 27 years old. There are 160 beds with rooms for two, four or six people. €14 per person per night from March through October, €13 from November through February. Breakfast and bed linen are included. ⓐ 10 rue Trousseau ⓣ 01 47 00 62 00 ⓦ www.aijparis.com ⓜ Metro: Ledru Rollin

**3 Ducks Hostel** Dormitories for four to eight persons. Prices from €16 to €23 per person per night (including breakfast). ⓐ 6 Place Etienne ⓣ 01 48 42 04 05 ⓦ www.3ducks.fr ⓜ Metro: Commerce

## CAMPING

**Camping du Bois de Boulogne** This is the only campsite within Paris. ⓐ 2 allée du Bord de l'Eau ⓣ 01 45 24 30 00 ⓦ www.campingparis.fr/boulogne.html

# THE BEST OF PARIS

In a city as rich in history, art, culture and architectural beauty as Paris, honing the choice experiences down to the top 10 is a challenge. However, here are those that, as the French say, are *les musts*. However much time you have, try to include a walk, either along the Seine, through the old district of the Marais, the Île-de-la-Cité and Île Saint-Louis or around Montmartre.

## TOP 10 ATTRACTIONS

- **Arc de Triomphe** Built to honour Napoleon's victories, this grand, angular arch stands in the centre of 12 avenues, the most famous of which is the Champs-Elysées (see pages 62–4).

- **Cimetière du Père-Lachaise** Probably the world's most famous cemetery, Père-Lachaise is the final, beautiful resting place of some of France's most illustrious figures from Balzac to Piaf (see pages 83–4).

- **Latin Quarter** This lively area is the heart of the Left Bank. Once famous for its students and literary legacy, it is now buzzing with cafés and bistros, nightclubs and chic boutiques (see page 102).

- **Markets** Integral to the daily life of Paris are its markets, from abundant fresh food markets to specialty markets selling anything from birds to bric-a-brac (see page 103).

- **Montmartre** Many visitors may know Montmartre through the movies, since this, and the adjacent Pigalle, is the famed historic, artistic area of the Moulin Rouge and the picturesque, magical world of Amélie Poulain (see pages 66–7).

- **Musée d'Orsay** The former 19th-century train station is now renowned for its collection of Western art from 1848 to 1914 (see pages 108–10).

- **Musée du Louvre** Once home of the kings of France, the 800-year-old Louvre could be called the king of museums, renowned the world over and housing works from ancient civilizations, the mid-1900s, and everything in between (see pages 67–9).

- **Notre-Dame** Like a silent sentinel, this magnificent Gothic cathedral on an island in the Seine has witnessed some of France's greatest events (see pages 85–6).

- **Seine** This aquatic artery meandering for 13 km (7½ miles) through Paris is the exquisite heart of the city (see pages 105–6).

- **Tour Eiffel** The graceful, filigreed metal tower, glowing burnished gold at night, is the symbol of France around the world (see page 106).

▼ *There's so much to experience in Paris*

## HALF-DAY: PARIS IN A HURRY

If you have only half a day in Paris, taking the Batobus (see page 106) the length of the Seine from the Notre-Dame to the Eiffel Tower or vice versa and visiting each monument at either end will give a compact, visually stunning introduction to Paris.

⬥ *Notre-Dame is beautiful from any angle*

## ONE DAY: TIME TO SEE A LITTLE MORE

As well as the Batobus or an hour-long tour on one of the many sightseeing boats, such as the Bateaux Parisiens (❶ 01 46 99 43 13 ⓦ www.bateauxparisiens.com), you should fit in a half-day tour of either the Musée du Louvre (see pages 67–9) or the Musée d'Orsay (see pages 108–10).

## 2–3 DAYS: SHORT CITY-BREAK

Adding to one of the above itineraries, climb to the top of the Arc de Triomphe (see pages 62–3) for a real perspective of the grand design of Paris, especially the broad boulevards stretching out like a star. A stroll down the Champs-Elysées, with its elegant shops and cafés, is a must. Over on the Left Bank, do as the Parisians do, visit a gallery or museum, then have a coffee at one of the famous literary cafés (see page 115), watching the *beau monde* go by and soaking up the ambience of the Latin Quarter.

## LONGER: ENJOYING PARIS TO THE FULL

Explore the *butte* (or hill) of Paris at Montmartre, where the Place du Tertre behind the white-domed Sacré-Coeur is the quintessential Parisian painters' corner. Licensed painters sell portraits or depictions of your favourite Parisian scene. From in front of the Sacré-Coeur, the rooftops of Paris stretch out below. Montmartre, with its climbing cobbled streets, is a great area to have a coffee or a meal.

If you have time to explore beyond Paris, you may wish to visit Versailles, the grand château and gardens built for Louis XIV, particularly if you can time your visit for the Grandes Eaux Musicales (see page 9) or the Fêtes de Nuit (see page 10). Other getaways are suggested in the 'Out of Town' section (see pages 121–38).

# Something for nothing

The best things in life may not all be free, but in seductive Paris many wonderful experiences are there for the asking. The national museums, for example, are free on the first Sunday of every month. These include the Louvre, the Musée d'Orsay, the Conciergerie, the Panthéon, the Musée National du Moyen Age (in the Thermes gallo-romains and the Hôtel de Cluny) and the Musée National des Arts Asiatiques-Guimet.

As well as these, the permanent collections of all Paris City Council museums are free. One of these, the charming Musée Carnavalet, displays the history of Paris from the French Revolution to today (ⓐ 23 rue de la Sevigne ⓣ 01 44 59 58 58 ⓦ www.carnavalet.paris.fr).

Also in the Marais district, which houses some of the oldest buildings in Paris, is the 17th-century Place des Vosges. Ruddy-pink brick pavilions form a handsome square that is both a peaceful public space and a collection of art galleries. Nobility and literary figures, such as the poet and novelist Victor Hugo, lived here and his house is now a museum (see page 84).

On the Left Bank, adjacent to the famous Sorbonne University, the Chapelle de la Sorbonne is one of Paris's lesser-known charms. Cool and calming, as befitting its spiritual nature, the chapel stages free exhibitions of art. (It is currently closed for repairs to its façade, which should be finished by mid-2007.)

Nearby, the fence along the famous Jardin du Luxembourg has become an outdoor photo gallery. Huge photographs, many by news photographers and photojournalists, engage and entertain passers-by. Expositions are rotated and each photo is lit at night, providing an enchanting night-time pastime.

During Paris's long, sultry summers, free concerts are held in some 20 parks and gardens and there is often a Latin or African drumbeat to be heard along the quays of central Paris.

The city itself is a walkable feast, and perhaps nowhere can you get more value for your nothing spent than strolling along the Seine. Each side of the river, from the Notre-Dame curving westward to the Eiffel Tower, provides a panorama of some of the world's most famous buildings and of the bridges that link Left Bank to Right.

◆ *View of Paris from the Seine banks*

# When it rains

Rainy days are no problem in Paris, filled as it is with so many wonderful museums in which to keep entertained and dry. Most museums are open through the weekend, closing on either Monday or Tuesday. Many, such as the Louvre, the Musée d'Orsay and the Maillol, have charming cafés to lounge in if your feet get tired.

● *Try the Rivoli restaurant in the BHV department store*

A particularly atmospheric retreat is the 5th-floor Rivoli restaurant in the BHV department store near the Hôtel de Ville. The Rivoli, with a simple, airy décor, serves light snacks and drinks, but its star attraction is the panoramic view of the Paris rooftops, particularly the Hôtel de Ville, the Panthéon and many old buildings with their mansard roofs and chimneypots.

Parisian cafés and brasseries are an integral part of the soul of the city. Simple, traditional establishments or fancier places with polished brass and wood fittings are wonderful places to escape the rain, relax and watch Paris life go by, while warmed by a *café crème* (coffee with frothed milk) or *chocolat chaud* (hot chocolate).

While non-smokers will likely be offended by the lack of non-smoking tables (but this is so French, isn't it?), the atmosphere in these traditional Paris venues usually offsets any discomfort.

One way to get an instant briefing on Paris on a rainy day is to catch a screening of the excellent film *Paris Story*. In this multimedia promenade through Paris's past, 2,000 years of history plays out on a giant screen, with the character of Victor Hugo narrating.

Even for non-shoppers, the glass-covered passages of Paris are a delightful legacy of the early 19th century. Originally constructed to protect shoppers from wet weather, they still do so today, while housing luxury goods and boutiques. Among the most charming of the remaining arcades are the Grand-Cerf at 145 rue Saint-Denis, with its designer boutiques, and the galeries Colbert and Vivienne, at 16 rue des Petits-Champs, known for book collections and haute couture. All three are in the 2nd *arrondissement*.

**Paris Story** ❷ 11 bis rue Scribe, 9th *arrondissement* ❶ 01 42 66 62 06 ⓦ www.exploreparis.fr ❶ shows on the hour 09.00–19.00 ⓝ Metro: Opéra

# On arrival

## TIME DIFFERENCES

France is on Central European Time (CET). During Daylight Saving
Time (late Mar–late Sept), the clocks are moved forward one hour.
At 12.00 in Paris in summer, times elsewhere are as follows:

**Australia** Eastern Standard Time 20.00, Central Standard Time 19.30,
Western Standard Time 18.00
**New Zealand** 22.00
**South Africa** 12.00
**UK** 11.00
**USA and Canada** Newfoundland Time 07.30, Atlantic Canada Time
07.00, Eastern Time 06.00, Central Time 05.00, Mountain Time
04.00, Pacific Time 03.00, Alaska 02.00

## ARRIVING

### By air

Paris has two main airports, Roissy-Charles de Gaulle (CDG), 23 km
(14¼ miles) north of the city, and Orly, 14 km (8½ miles) south.

The easiest way to the city centre from both Charles de Gaulle
and Orly airports for those travelling light is by RER B commuter
train. The line goes to Gare du Nord, Châtelet (centre of the Right
Bank) and Saint-Michel (Left Bank). There are metro connections
from those stations.

Those with more luggage can take Air France buses, which leave
every 15 minutes to Porte Maillot and Charles de Gaulle-Etoile in
Paris. There is also a service to the train stations of Gare de Lyon and
Gare Montparnasse (ⓦ www.cars-airfrance.com). The RATP also
operates bus services: the Roissybus to rue Scribe (behind Palais

Garnier) and the Orlybus to Denfert-Rochereau. These operate about every 20 minutes (W www.ratp.fr).

The most comfortable (and expensive) way to get to the city is by taxi, available outside the arrivals terminal. From the CDG airport to the centre of Paris will cost about €50 to €60, but could be higher during rush hours and traffic jams. There is a surcharge after 19.00, on Sundays and on holidays. Many drivers don't speak much English, so have your destination address written out. Taxis from Orly will be about €35 to €60 with normal traffic conditions. Drivers usually charge a fee for bags. Avoid touts inside the airport offering taxi or limousine service, as you will invariably end up paying much more. Go to the taxi ranks outside the terminal instead.

Several companies provide a minivan service, with delivery to hotels, but you have to book in advance, and you may have to share with other passengers. For information on this, check www.parisinfo.com

Some charter airlines, and Ryanair, use Beauvais airport, which is quite far from the city. Buses leave from the airport parking lot to the city. You can also use a combination of taxi and train to get to Gare du Nord. For return flights, buses leave from Hôtel Concorde Lafayette. You need to get to the hotel three-and-a-quarter hours before your flight departure time.

**Roissy-Charles de Gaulle** and **Orly** W www.adp.fr
**Beauvais** W www.aeroportbeauvais.com

**By rail**
Those travelling on Eurostar from Britain arrive at Gare du Nord. From here, RER B goes into the city (central stations are Châtelet and Saint-Michel). Alternatively, there is a taxi stand at the right-hand side of the station after disembarking the Eurostar.

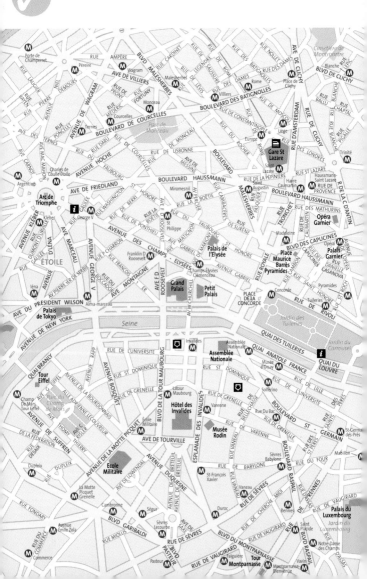

**BY ROAD**

It isn't ad
hectic
park

ısable driving into, or around, Paris. Traffic is heavy and
ᵤarking spaces are hard to find (unless the hotel has a car
 and the one-way systems can be complex.

If you still wish to drive, the main roads into Paris all reach the
*périphérique* (ring road), which has various exits to different parts of
the city. Those arriving from the UK by car will probably use the A1
from the north.

Despite competition from the Chunnel, ferry and hydrofoil
services, most taking cars as well as passengers, continue to operate
across the English Channel (*la Manche*, the sleeve, to the French) day
and night in all seasons.

## FINDING YOUR FEET

Tourist office welcome centres at Gare du Nord, Pyramides, Opéra,
Gare de Lyon and the Tour Eiffel provide free maps in ten languages.
The telephone answering service is available 24 hours a day on
08 92 68 30 00.

All hotels provide good complimentary maps featuring streets as
well as the metro system. Be sure to get the hotel's *carte de visite*
(business card) and keep it with you in case you get lost.

The best way to get to know Paris is to walk around the hotel
neighbourhood. Paris is like a series of villages, each with its own
attraction and character. Then you can begin to explore further
afield by public transport.

### Crime & safety

Violent crime is rare, but there are many pickpockets in Paris,
especially on the metro during rush hours and at crowded tourist
sites. Leave valuables, extra cash, jewellery, passports and other

valuables in the hotel or room safe. Always be vigilant and keep bags and wallets closed and out of reach. Don't be obvious, carrying big bulky cameras and purses, which will attract pickpockets.

Always go to an official sales point to buy tickets, and avoid touts. If you encounter any problems, look for a uniformed police officer, transport security staff or ticket sales staff.

## ORIENTATION

Paris is divided into 20 *arrondissement*s (districts). The 1st is the centre of the city, and the others are laid out in a clockwise spiral from there. The Seine divides the city into Left and Right Banks. As the *arrondissements* are so basic to the layout of Paris, they are constantly referred to in guides and literature, almost always using simply their associated number (1st, 2nd, etc.).

The main city thoroughfares include the Champs-Elysées and boulevard Haussmann on the Right Bank, and boulevard Saint-Germain and Saint-Michel on the Left.

Paris is a small city, easy to navigate on foot. You can walk across it from east to west or north to south in one day, if you don't stop for sightseeing. However, it is not always pedestrian-friendly, so it is important to be alert, especially at crossings.

If you get lost, go down into a metro and find your way on a map. Some metro stops have maps displaying the immediate area. You can also get your bearings from the Eiffel Tower, Arc de Triomphe, Panthéon, Notre-Dame or Tour Montparnasse.

## GETTING AROUND

Local transport systems are excellent and inexpensive.

Paris has an excellent metro system reaching all parts of the city. It is the main, most efficient way to get around. The 14 lines

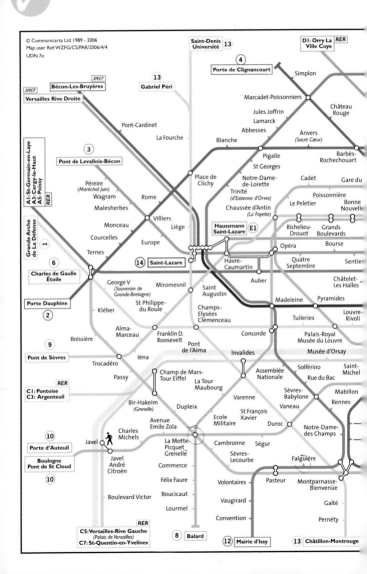

© Communicarta Ltd 1989 - 2006
Map user Ref:WZFG/CS/PAR/2006/4/4
UDN.7e

Saint-Denis Université **13**

DI: Orry La Ville Coye *RER*

*SNCF*
Bécon-Les-Bruyères

Gabriel Péri **13**

**4** Porte de Clignancourt

Simplon

*SNCF*
Versailles Rive Droite

Marcadet-Poissonniers

Château Rouge

Pont-Cardinet

Jules Joffrin
Lamarck
Abbesses

**3**

La Fourche

Blanche

Anvers
(Sacré Cœur)

Barbès-Rochechouart

Pont de Levallois-Bécon

Péreire
(Maréchal Juin)
Wagram

Place de Clichy

Pigalle

St Georges

Cadet

Gare du

Notre-Dame-de-Lorette

Poissonnière

A1: St-Germain-en-Laye
A3: Cergy-le-Haut
A5: Poissy

Rome
Maleshesbes

Trinité
(d'Estienne d'Orves)

Le Peletier

Bonne Nouvelle

*RER*

Monceau
Courcelles

Villiers

Liège

Chaussée d'Antin
(La Fayette)

Haussmann
Saint-Lazare **E1**

Richelieu-Drouot

Grands Boulevards

Grande Arche de La Défense

Ternes

Europe

Opéra

Bourse

**1**

**14** Saint-Lazare

Havre-Caumartin

Sentier

**6**
Charles de Gaulle Étoile

George V
(Souverain de Grande-Bretagne)

Miromesnil

Saint Augustin

Quatre Septembre

Châtelet-Les Halles

Porte Dauphine

**2**

Kléber

St Philippe-du Roule

Champs-Elysées Clémenceau

Madeleine

Pyramides

Tuileries

Louvre-Rivoli

Alma-Marceau

Franklin D. Roosevelt

Concorde

Palais-Royal Musée du Louvre

**9**

Boissière

Iéna

Pont de l'Alma

Musée d'Orsay

Pont de Sèvres

Trocadéro

Invalides

Assemblée Nationale

Solférino

Saint-Michel

*RER*

Passy

Champ de Mars-Tour Eiffel

La Tour Maubourg

Rue du Bac

C1: Pontoise
C3: Argenteuil

Bir-Hakeim
(Grenelle)

Dupleix

Varenne

Sèvres-Babylone

Mabillon

St François Xavier

Vaneau

Rennes

Avenue Emile Zola

Ecole Militaire

Duroc

Notre-Dame-des Champs

**10**
Porte d'Auteuil

Javel

Charles Michels

La Motte-Picquet Grenelle

Cambronne

Ségur

Falguière

Boulogne Pont de St Cloud

Javel André Citroën

Commerce

Sèvres-Lecourbe

**10**

Félix Faure

Volontaires

Pasteur

Montparnasse-Bienvenüe

Boulevard Victor

Boucicaut

Vaugirard

Gaîté

Lourmel

Convention

Pernéty

*RER*
C5:Versailles-Rive Gauche
(Palais de Versailles)
C7: St-Quentin-en-Yvelines

**8** Balard

**12** Mairie d'Issy

**13** Châtillon-Montrouge

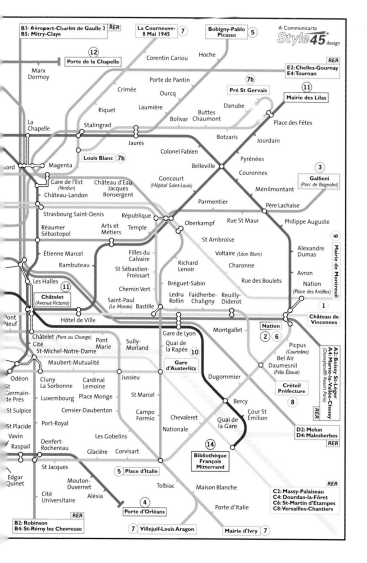

## IF YOU GET LOST, TRY …

**Excuse me, do you speak English?**
Excusez-moi, vous parlez anglais?
*Ekskeweh mwah, voopahrlay ahnglay?*

**Excuse me, is this the right way to the old town/the city centre/the tourist office/the station/the bus station?**
Excusez-moi, c'est la bonne direction pour la vieille ville/au centre-ville/l'office de tourisme/la gare/la gare routière?
*Ekskewzaymwah, seh lah bon deerekseeawng poor lah veeay veel/ oh sahngtr veel/lohfeece de tooreezm/lah gahr/lah gahr rootyair?*

**Can you point to it on my map?**
Pouvez-vous me le montrer sur la carte?
*Poovehvoo mer ler mawngtreh sewr lah kart?*

are identified by number and colour. The RER commuter trains connect to the suburbs. An RATP 'Paris Visite' is a travel pass for one, two, three or five consecutive days on metro, bus and RER trains, including to the airport. A one-day adult pass for one to three zones is €8.35; a five-day pass for the same zones is €26.65. The pass is worth purchasing only if you plan to move around the city a lot. A single €1.40 metro ticket can be used for one journey by metro, train or bus in zones one and two, including all connections. Tickets can be purchased singly or in a carnet (book) of ten for €10.50 at the ticket offices or machines in metro stations, and also in some tobacconists. Keep your ticket until you have completed your journey; on the RER you will need it to exit the system. Note that the entire Paris metro network is a no-smoking zone.

Bus routes are more difficult to work out, but buses are more fun to ride. Route maps are available free in metro stations.

You can hail taxis in the street or at taxi ranks. Meters start at €2 or €3, more if you pre-order a taxi. If you want a receipt, ask for *un reçu*.

▲ *Metropolitan underground station*

SNCF trains to out-of-town areas depart from these *gares* (stations): Gare du Nord, Gare de l'Est, St Lazare, Lyon, Austerlitz and Montparnasse.

**RATP** provides information in English on buses, metro and RER commuter trains ☎ 08 92 68 41 14 🌐 www.ratp.com

**SNCF** ☎ 01 53 90 20 20 🌐 www.sncf.fr

## CAR HIRE

It is not a good idea to rent a car to use in Paris or to get to out-of-town places. For travelling around Île-de-France or throughout the country, it is better to take the excellent, efficient SNCF trains and hire a car at your destination. For information, see www.sncf.com

If you do wish to hire a car in Paris, you will find all the major car-rental companies here, all with offices at Charles de Gaulle airport. Rates range from about €30 a day up to more than €100. They are reliable, but you should make sure you have adequate insurance.

**Avis** ☎ 01 48 62 59 59 🌐 www.avis.com

**Europcar** ☎ 01 56 08 05 15 🌐 www.europcar.com

**Hertz** ☎ 01 43 22 58 69 🌐 www.hertz.com

**National** ☎ 01 47 07 87 39 🌐 www.nationalcar.com

**Thrifty** ☎ 01 43 47 58 80 🌐 www.thrifty.com

### PARIS THROUGH THE MOVIES

Commercial cinema was born in the City of Light, when brothers Louis and Auguste Lumière projected their first films in the basement of the Grand Café on the boulevard des Capucines on 28 December, 1895. Since then, more than 400 major motion pictures have been shot among Paris's cobbled alleys, stone squares, tree-lined boulevards and broad quays, making it among the world's most filmed capitals.

Many films depict the clichéd Paris of accordion music, pungent Gauloise cigarettes, the cancan, *flics* (French policemen) and Inspector Clouseau. Most include a view of Gustave Eiffel's imposing wrought-iron tower, the city's most famous landmark. Another popular backdrop, the Seine, is familiar to movie fans worldwide. In the zany 1965 spectacle *What's New, Pussycat?*, Woody Allen celebrates his birthday by setting up a table and chairs on the quay.

Marlon Brando pursued Maria Schneider along the twin-decked Bir-Hakeim Bridge in Bernardo Bertolucci's darkly erotic *Last Tango in Paris* (1972). More recently, Robert Altman's 1994 *Prêt-à-Porter* displays a less glamorous view of the city, with its traffic jams, rain and grey skies – and the dog droppings on so many streets. But it also shows an idyllic, tourist-video vision of Paris, with a view of the sun rising over the Haussmann rooftops, the noble Notre-Dame cathedral, a dazzling night view of the Arc de Triomphe and the glamorous Champs-Elysées.

The 1963 comedy *Irma la Douce* played out around the less glamorous giant food markets, Les Halles, the 'belly of Paris'. The markets moved out of central Paris in 1969.

Part of *What's New, Pussycat?* is set north of here, in and around the Crazy Horse strip club, where Allen, as the concupiscent Victor Skakapopulis, works as an 'undresser'.

Numerous movies are set in the clubs of racy *fin-de-siècle* Paris. The 1952 *Moulin Rouge*, with Zsa Zsa Gabor as Jane Avril and José Ferrer as poster boy Toulouse-Lautrec, evokes the

Belle Epoque ambience and freneticism of Paris's zesty, raunchy nightlife. It planted images of skirt-hoisting cancan dancers, Champagne and absinthe (the 'Green Fairy'), smoky cabarets, accordion players and slinky *chanteuses* in many impressionable minds. However, the latest musical offering of *Moulin Rouge* (2001), with Nicole Kidman and Ewan McGregor, takes place in a computer-generated Paris, created in a studio. Despite the actors' lively performances, the digitised Paris offers viewers no real feel of the city or of the legendary club.

The popular French hit of 2001, *Amélie from Montmartre*, takes place in a *moulin* of a different sort a few minutes' walk from the infamous club. In that colourful district in the north of the city, Amélie works and devises her altruistic schemes at the Café Tabac des Deux Moulins on 15 rue Lepic, now on many a cinephile's must-see list. The bar, with a poster of the impish heroine in one corner, looks smaller than in the movie, but does have the old Paris ambience. The rest of the lively *quartier* is also recognisable, though in a slightly less pristine state; the Art Nouveau Abbesses metro station, the antique carousel in Place St-Pierre and the greengrocer on Lepic are all now pasted with *Amélie* clippings.

Paris seems so familiar. It's all been seen before – at the movies.

● *Paris has a variety of architectural styles*

# Right Bank West

The traditional separation of Paris into Left and Right Bank, between business and culture, is no longer valid. The Left Bank still has most of the universities (especially the Sorbonne) and the bohemian cafés, but today the Right Bank also has artistic areas, especially the Marais and the Bastille. Both sides of the Seine have their distinct charm and attractions. For ease of sightseeing, we have divided the city into three areas: Right Bank West, Right Bank East and Left Bank.

Under the direction of Napoleon III, Baron Georges Haussmann reshaped and modernised Paris. His work is most obvious in this area of the city, with its broad, tree-lined boulevards, magnificent monuments, grand mansions and open gardens. Some of the city's greatest sights are found on the Right Bank West, such as the Louvre, the Champs-Elysées and Arc de Triomphe, Montmartre and Sacré-Coeur.

## SIGHTS & ATTRACTIONS

### Arc de Triomphe

Built to honour Napoleon's victories, this grand arch is the centrepiece of 12 boulevards that radiate 360 degrees from it. Stairs lead 50 m (164 ft) up to its roof for a panoramic view of the symmetry of Paris. La Voie Royale runs from the Louvre to the modern Grande Arche in the Place de la Défense. Beneath the Arc de Triomphe, a flame burns for an unknown soldier from World War I. There is a flame-tending ceremony every evening at 18.00. There's free admission on the first Sunday of the month during winter.
ⓐ Place du Général-de-Gaulle ⓣ 01 55 37 73 77 ⓦ www.monum.fr

🕐 10.00–23.00 (summer); 10.00–22.30 (winter) Ⓜ Metro: Charles de Gaulle Etoile ❶ closed on all major public holidays

### Champs-Elysées

Many songs have been written about the Champs-Elysées, the grandest of boulevards stretching away from the Arc de Triomphe. Wandering down this great thoroughfare, you may feel rather privileged and free, as the folk-singer Joni Mitchell sang in her famous lyrics: 'I was a free man in Paris...' Luxury boutiques and car showrooms, nightclubs and the *beau monde* are all here. Having a coffee on 'the Champs' isn't cheap, but the passing parade is worth the price. At night, with the Arc floodlit in golden light, the Champs is certainly impressive. However, despite the boulevard's grand demeanor, not all prices are grand. There are some pizzerias and burger bars for those on a budget.

Ⓜ Metro: Charles de Gaulle Etoile

### Conciergerie

One of the oldest buildings in Paris, the conical-towered Conciergerie on the Île-de-la-Cité, once a palace, became a prison during the French Revolution. Among the 2,800 prisoners held here, the most famous was Marie-Antoinette, who was taken to the guillotine at Place de la Concorde. Her cell can be seen today. Guided visits are available.

🅐 2 boulevard du Palais ☎ 01 53 40 60 80 🆆 www.monum.fr

🕐 09.30–18.00 (summer); 09.00–17.00 (winter) Ⓜ Metro: Cité

### Jardin des Tuileries

Declared a UNESCO World Heritage Site, the Tuileries, Paris's oldest park, forms an orderly sweep of greenery, gardens and statuary leading up to the Louvre and affording wonderful views of the museum buildings in one direction and the Arc de Triomphe in the other. Children sail miniature boats in the *bassins* (ponds), while adults hang out at cafés under the trees (including limes, rare elms and chestnuts). The park, a haven in hot summers, is also a sculpture garden, with works by Rodin, Henry Moore and Max Ernst, among others. A recent sculpture addition, loved by the birds, is Giuseppe Penone's *Arbre des Yoyelles*, a bronze fallen tree. At its western end, the park is graced by the exposition spaces Galerie Nationale du Jeu de Paume (www.jeudepaume.org) and the Musée de l'Orangerie

◆ *A building on one of Haussmann's boulevards*

(www.musee-orangerie.fr), scheduled to open in late 2006.
🕐 07.30–21.00 (summer); 07.30–19.30 (winter) Ⓜ Metro: Tuileries

## Montmartre

This historic district in the 18th *arrondissement*, called the 'balcony of Paris', is characterised by the white-domed Sacré-Coeur at its heart, steep streets lined with ancient buildings, and a lively buzz from the tourists and locals congregating at terrace cafés, restaurants, crowded boutiques and around the basilica. This is the area immortalised by Toulouse-Lautrec in his paintings and posters of the Moulin Rouge and saucy cancan girls. The Moulin Rouge, circa 1889, is still lively, these days with tall, leggy Australian and Scandinavian girls strutting their stuff. Nearby Pigalle, which American soldiers dubbed 'Pig Alley', advertises in loud neon its sex shows and wares. This is also the Paris of *Amélie*, from the recent film of the same name (see 'Paris through the movies', pages 58–60). Like a cartoon train, the little white Montmartrain tootles through the cobbled streets of Montmartre, giving commentary in several languages. It departs in front of the Sacré-Coeur or the Place Pigalle.

Crowning Montmartre with white cupolas, the basilica of **Sacré-Coeur** is one of the most visible of Paris's landmarks. It is especially beautiful on bright, blue days or glowing pearl-white at night, but insiders say the stone is loveliest glistened with rain. Those with the energy can climb up the main rotunda. At weekends, especially in summer, the steps and grounds of the basilica are crowded with sightseers, entertained by an assortment of performers and buskers.

The **Place du Tertre** is an ancient square just west of the Sacré-Coeur and is the quintessential artists-with-easel scene, sitting on the very 'rooftop' of Paris. Its picture-postcard ambience has made it crowded, though, so you may have to take a rest in one of the neighbourhood cafés or wine bars. There is even a Montmartre wine, and a tiny vineyard nearby (between rue des Saules and rue Saint-Vincent).

If you're hanging out for some retail therapy, boutiques in the **Place des Abbesses**, west of the Sacré-Coeur, have a relaxed atmosphere on Sundays, when most Paris shops are closed.
**Sacré-Coeur** ❷ 35 rue du Chevalier-de-la-Barre ❶ 01 53 41 89 00 🕙 basilica 06.00–23.00; dome and crypt 09.00–17.45 Ⓜ Metro: Anvers or Abbesses

### Musée du Louvre

One of the world's largest museums, the Musée du Louvre exhibits only 10 per cent of its priceless works. It is renowned for such masterpieces as the *Mona Lisa*, affectionately called 'La Joconde' by the French, the *Venus de Milo*, *Winged Victory*, *Psyche and Cupid*, Da Vinci's *Virgin and Child with St Anne* and Géricault's *Raft of the Medusa*. With some eight departments and some 35,000 works on display, the Louvre could be daunting to those trying to take in its immensity of riches. Yet rooms with polished wood floors and warm lighting are immediately inviting. You can get up close and personal to some of your favourite works and gaze from central benches when you get weary. The best approach is to pick a favourite period and hone in on that. You won't see it all, so relax and enjoy. The wonders that you do see will provide a lifetime of memories.

Even if you're not visiting the Louvre, you can walk through Passage Richelieu off the rue de Rivoli to view some of the museum's wondrous marble and bronze sculptures through large windows. Upon entering the central courtyard, the Cour Napoléon, you'll see I M Pei's *Pyramid du Louvre* of glass and rivets. This modern structure, which is the museum's main entrance, has provoked considerable controversy, with many complaining that it spoiled the symmetry of the old buildings. Yet with the ancient structures reflected in the modern one and fountains further softening the

● *Go inside to view the treasures of the Louvre*

transition, most visitors feel that the effect is a harmonious juxtaposition of palace and pyramid.

ⓐ rue de Rivoli ⓣ 01 40 20 50 50 ⓛ 09.00–18.00 (until 21.45 Wed & Fri), closed Tues ⓝ Metro: Palais Royal Musée du Louvre

---

**LOUVRE TIPS**

To avoid the queues, buy advance tickets from such outlets as FNAC and Virgin stores.

Late opening nights have reduced rates and the first Sunday of the month is free.

Da Vinci Code tours, based on sights mentioned in Dan Brown's book, are among the most popular in Paris.

---

### Place de la Concorde

The golden-tipped obelisk in the centre of the square is actually a 3,200-year-old Egyptian relic from Luxor. This bright grand square has a bloody history: during the French Revolution, more than 1,000 people were guillotined here, including King Louis XVI and Marie-Antoinette.

ⓝ Metro: Concorde

### Sainte-Chapelle

This delicate gem among Paris churches is renowned for its 13th-century stained-glass windows, whose 15-m (49-ft) compositions captivate onlookers and fill the chapel with jewels of light.

ⓐ 4 boulevard du Palais ⓣ 01 53 40 60 80 ⓦ www.monum.fr
ⓛ 09.30–18.00 (summer); 09.00–17.00 (winter) ⓝ Metro: Cité

### Tenniseum

The Stade Roland-Garros, where the French Open is held, is open for visits when there are no games. The first multimedia tennis museum, the Tenniseum covers some 2,200 sq m (23,681 sq ft). There are also guided tours of the museum and stadium.
ⓐ 2 avenue Gordon-Bennett ⓣ 01 47 43 48 48 ⓦ www.fft.fr or www.rolandgarros.com ⓛ 10.00–18.00, closed Mon
ⓜ Metro: Porte d'Auteuil

### Trocadéro

A half-moon shaped structure on the Right Bank facing the Eiffel Tower, the Palais de Chaillot, called the Trocadéro, was built for the 1937 Exposition Universelle. It houses the Musée de l'Homme (ⓣ 01 44 05 72 72 ⓦ www.mnhn.fr), le Musée National de la Marine (ⓣ 01 53 65 69 69 ⓦ www.musee-marine.fr) and the Théâtre National de Chaillot (ⓣ 01 53 65 30 00 ⓦ www.theatre-chaillot.fr). Also opening in the Trocadéro in late 2006 is the new Cité de l'Architecture et du Patrimoine (www.citechaillot.org).
In summer, people chill out around the Trocadéro's cool pools and lawns. The central square, where the wings of the building cleave in two, reveals a magnificent, full frontal view of the Eiffel Tower.
ⓐ 17 Place du Trocadéro ⓜ Metro: Trocadéro

## CULTURE

### Galeries Nationales du Grand Palais

With its splendid Belle Epoque glass roof visible along the Seine's right bank, this grand palace built for the 1900 World Fair holds major art expositions.

📍 3 avenue du General Eisenhower ☎ 01 44 13 1/17
🌐 www.rmn.fr/galeriesnationalesdugrandpalais 🕐 10.00–20.00,
until 22.00 Wed, closed Tues Ⓜ Metro: Champs-Elysées Clémenceau

### Musée Dapper

This small, intimate space displays African art, from sub-Sahara to
the diasporas of the continent.
📍 35 rue Paul Valéry ☎ 01 45 00 91 75 🕐 11.00–19.00, closed Tues, free
admission on the last Wed of the month Ⓜ Metro: Victor Hugo

### Musée d'Art Moderne de la Ville de Paris

After two years of renovation, the city's modern art museum is open
anew with such important expositions as a retrospective of Pierre
Bonnard. Next door, the Palais de Tokyo (☎ 01 47 23 38 86
🕐 12.00–midnight, closed Mon) is a grand display case for
contemporary art. 📍 11 avenue du President Wilson ☎ 01 53 67 40 00
🌐 www.paris.fr/musees 🕐 10.00–18.00, until 22.00 Wed, closed Mon
Ⓜ Metro: Iéna

### Musée du Vieux Montmartre

This is a hidden treasure in a charming 17th-century building
entered through a small courtyard. The artists Duffy, Utrillo and
Renoir lived and worked here.
📍 12 rue Cortot ☎ 01 46 06 61 11 🕐 10.00–18.00, closed Mon
Ⓜ Metro: Lamarck-Caulaincourt

### Musée Marmottan Monet

This lovely museum, in what was once a private home, houses a
large collection of Impressionists, among other works, particularly
the *Water Lilies* and other masterpieces of Claude Monet.

ⓐ 2 rue Louis-Boilly ⓣ 01 44 96 50 33 ⓦ www.marmottan.com
ⓛ 10.00–18.00, closed Mon ⓜ Metro: La Muette

**Musée National des Arts Asiatiques–Guimet**
Renovations to the building around five years ago brought light and volume to one of the world's best collections of Asian art. Some 45,000 objects include works from China, Japan, India and Southeast Asia. Its annex, the **Panthéon Bouddhique**, is a little-known jewel with ancient Buddhist statues, a Japanese garden and tea pavilion. The garden, a tiny oasis, has stands of bamboo, trickling waterfalls, wooden walkways and flowers changed each season.
**Musée Guimet** ⓐ 6 Place d'Iena ⓣ 01 56 52 53 00
ⓦ www.museeguimet.fr ⓛ 10.00–17.45 Wed–Mon ⓜ Metro: Iéna
**Panthéon Bouddhique** ⓐ 19 avenue d'Iena ⓣ 01 40 73 88 00
ⓛ 09.45–17.45, closed Tues ⓜ Metro: Iéna

**Palais Garnier: Opéra National de Paris**
Built on the orders of Napoleon III, the Palais Garnier, with its grand façade and foyer (both recently renovated), is a masterpiece of 19th-century design. It was designed by Charles Garnier to resemble a classical château. With its sweeping marble staircase, mirrors and gilded mosaics in the grand foyer, sculptures and painted ceiling depicting allegories of music, this awe-inspiring building is one of the most visited in Paris. The horseshoe-shaped auditorium has a ceiling painted by Marc Chagall. It offers a full programme of dance, ballet and opera year-round, except August.
ⓐ Place de l'Opéra ⓣ 08 92 89 90 90, guided visit bookings 01 41 10 08 10 ⓦ www.operadeparis.fr ⓛ unaccompanied visits of the main areas 10.00–17.00, comprehensive guided visits last 90 minutes
ⓜ Metro: Opéra

**Petit Palais**

Recently reopened after four years of renovation, the city's sumptuous fine arts museum, circa 1900, contains the spectrum of art from antiquities to early 20th century. There are also excellent temporary exhibitions.

ⓐ avenue Winston Churchill ❶ 01 53 43 40 00
ⓦ www.petitpalais.paris.fr ❶ 10.00–18.00 Tues–Sun, until 21.00 Tues for temporary shows ⓝ Metro: Champs-Elysées Clémenceau

## RETAIL THERAPY

The Golden Triangle of haute couture is here, extending from the Faubourg Saint-Honoré, the Place Vendôme and the rue Royale, to the rue Montaigne and the Champs-Elysées. Fashion boutiques in rue Etienne Marcel, in the 1st and 2nd *arrondissements*, have become recently hip with the showbiz set.

**Carrousel du Louvre** The inverted glass pyramid of the Louvre (which fascinates kids, by the way) adds light and design drama to the Carrousel du Louvre. With its 45 boutiques and 14 restaurants, shoppers can keep occupied for hours. Goods range from fashion and jewellery to household items. Entrance on Rivoli, through the museum or the metro. ⓐ 99 rue de Rivoli ❶ 08.30–23.00, stores 07.00–20.00 ⓝ Metro: Palais Royal Musée du Louvre

**Colette** Probably the hippest boutique in town, with accessories, bling, CDs, clothes, tech toys and trinkets for the seriously fashionable. Here, you're likely to hear young French say, 'Oh, c'est cool'. There's a water bar downstairs with designer *eau* and a resident dog. ⓐ 213 rue Saint-Honoré

📞 01 55 35 33 90  🌐 www.colette.fr  🕐 11.00–19.00 Mon–Sat
🚇 Metro: Tuileries

**Custo Barcelona** Known for its cute t-shirts for guys and girls, in warm Mediterranean colours and with such designs as sequined words and caricatures... it's the t-shirt as canvas. It's pricey though, so you may choose to just window shop. There are several stores in Paris; we've listed the most recent. 📍 316 rue Saint-Honoré

🔺 *Not all of the city's fashion outlets specialise in haute couture*

🕿 01 42 60 02 36 🌐 www.custo-barcelona.com 🕐 11.00–19.00 Mon–Sat Ⓜ Metro: Tuileries

**Fauchon** Taking up two corners of the Place de la Madeleine and with shops all over town, Fauchon is perhaps the most elegant gourmet food store in Paris, selling fine foods from chocolates and foie gras to teas since 1886. A mini rose-coloured bag with two chocolates will give friends back home a taste of Paris. 🅐 26 Place de la Madeleine 🕿 01 70 39 38 00 🕐 09.00–21.00 Ⓜ Metro: Madeleine

**Forum des Halles** A sprawling subterranean shopping and cinema complex in the 1st *arrondissement*, this place buzzes with young shoppers and hangers-round, but the crowds can be crushing. The whole complex is set to be redesigned. Ⓜ Metro: Châtelet; RER: Châtelet Les Halles

**Galeries Lafayette** In the Opéra district, this elegant Parisian department store has designer duds, a new activewear department, a children's 'concept store', a separate building for men and a gourmet food section. The new Lafayette Maison across the street (No 35) has everything for the home. 🅐 40 boulevard Haussmann 🕿 01 42 82 34 56 🌐 www.galerieslafayette.com 🕐 09.30–19.30, until 21.00 Thur Ⓜ Metro: Chaussée-d'Antin-Lafayette

**Marché aux Puces de la Porte de Clignacourt** You can find some gems tucked among the junk at this huge flea market, which extends beyond the *périphérique* (ring road) into Saint-Ouen. 🅐 avenue de la Porte de Clignacourt 🕿 01 53 57 42 63 🌐 www.parispuces.com 🕐 09.00–19.00 Sat, Sun & Mon Ⓜ Metro: Porte de Clignacourt

**Printemps** A department store near Galeries Lafayette that also stocks a wide variety of fashionable clothes and accessories. 64 boulevard Haussmann 01 42 82 50 00 www.printemps.fr 09.35–19.00, until 22.00 Thur Metro: Hauvre-Caumartin

**Zara** With some 25 locations around Paris, this Spanish clothing store has copies of runway fashions at affordable prices. Items for men and children, too. 2 rue Halévy 01 44 71 90 90 10.00–20.00 Mon–Sat Metro: Opéra

## TAKING A BREAK

**Angelina £** ❶ This elegant patisserie and tea salon has a fin-de-siècle dining room as frothy as the pastries, including Baba au fruits and Mont Blanc. Its hot chocolate is legendary. 226 rue de Rivoli 01 42 60 82 00 08.00–19.00 Mon–Fri, 09.00–19.00 Sat & Sun Metro: Tuileries

**Cafés et Thés Verlet £** ❷ Founded in 1880, this cosy café features mirrors and old wood furnishings, burlap sacks of coffee beans and large old tea tins. You can purchase tea or coffee to take away or enjoy them on the premises with such delights as fruit crumble. 256 rue Saint-Honoré 01 42 60 67 39 09.30–18.30 Mon–Sat Metro: Pyramides

**Ladurée £** ❸ This celebrated tea salon (established 1862) is known for its excellent pastries and ornate dining room with painted ceiling of maidens and cherubs. Famous for its melt-in-your-mouth macaroons flavoured with pistachio, coffee, chocolate, lemon or strawberry. Four locations. 16 rue Royale

🕿 01 42 60 21 79 🕒 08.30–19.00 Mon–Sat, 10.00–19.00 Sun
Ⓜ Metro: Madeleine

**Le Progrès £** ❹ A simple café and bistro in Montmartre, with friendly staff and big picture windows from which to see the spires of the Sacré-Coeur peeking above the old buildings. Nice place to have a coffee or something stronger. ❸ 7 rue des Trois Frères
🕿 01 42 64 07 37 🕒 09.00–02.00 Ⓜ Metro: Anvers

## AFTER DARK

### Restaurants
**Aux Vieux Châtelet £** ❺ This traditional café-brasserie has a view of the river and some of the city's oldest buildings, like the Conciergerie and the Notre-Dame, dramatically illuminated at night. Simple French fare at reasonable prices. ❸ 1 Place du Châtelet
🕿 01 42 33 79 27 🕒 07.00–23.30 Ⓜ Metro: Châtelet

**Bouillon Chartier £** ❻ Since 1896, this traditional French bistro has offered standard French fare in a crowded, high-ceilinged room. The food can be hit and miss, but the lively, old-fashioned atmosphere is the main attraction. ❸ 7 rue Faubourg Montmartre 🕿 01 47 70 86 29
🕒 11.30–15.00 & 18.00–22.00 Ⓜ Metro: Grands Boulevards ❶ tables cannot be booked, so you may have to queue on arrival

**La Crypte Polska £** ❼ Ever dined in the crypt of a church? This one, in the basement of a Polish church, sells such hearty Polish fare as pork and cabbage dishes at reasonable prices. ❸ Place Maurice Barrès 🕿 01 42 60 43 33 🕒 12.00–15.00 Mon, 12.00–15.00 & 19.00–22.00 Tues–Sun Ⓜ Metro: Pyramides

**Café Marly ££** ❽   In the Louvre, a *branché* (trendy) café-restaurant, serving modern fare with a view of the sculptures and the glass pyramid. ⓐ 93 rue de Rivoli ❶ 01 49 26 06 60 ⏰ 08.00–02.00 Ⓝ Metro: Palais Royal Musée du Louvre

**Chez Vong ££** ❾   Perhaps the best of the city's good Chinese restaurants, this establishment near the Pompidou Centre has an authentic Chinese décor, excellent food (especially the seafood), attentive service and a refined atmosphere. ⓐ 10 rue de la Grande-Truanderie ❶ 01 40 26 09 36 ⏰ 12.00–14.30 & 19.00–midnight Mon–Sat Ⓝ Metro: Les Halles

**L'Angle Du Faubourg ££–£££** ❿   Local food critics rave about this place, with its authentic, well-prepared French fare such as succulent lamb and veal. ⓐ 195 rue du Faubourg Saint-Honoré ❶ 01 40 74 20 20 ⏰ closed weekends and Aug Ⓝ Metro: Charles de Gaulle-Etoile or Ternes

**Man Ray £££** ⓫   This fashionable night spot (also now known as Mandala Ray), named for the former avant-garde American artist/photographer in Paris, is one of the city's hottest. Celebrities Sean Penn and Johnny Depp are part owners. Décor in the spacious, two-storey bar/club/restaurant is Oriental, the cuisine is fusion, and the action is hot late at night, with a young, hip clientele. The ambience rates higher than the food and as the place never closes, you'll have ample time to appreciate both. ⓐ 34 rue Marbeuf ❶ 01 43 59 05 14 Ⓝ Metro: Franklin D Roosevelt

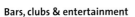

## Bars, clubs & entertainment

**Buddha Bar** The star attraction in this fashionable bar is its giant, golden Buddha presiding over the cool cocktail bar and restaurant. ⓐ 8 rue Boissy d'Anglas ⓣ 01 53 05 90 00 ⓛ weekdays for lunch, then daily from 16.00 Ⓜ Metro: Concorde

**Les Bains Douches** This former bathhouse turned dance club has attained mythical status on the Parisian nightclub circuit. ⓐ 7 rue du Bourg-l'Abbé ⓣ 01 48 87 01 80 ⓦ www.lesbainsdouches.net Ⓜ Metro: Elienne Marcel

**Le Bar du Plaza** Among the young French designers putting their distinctive stamp on Paris is Patrick Jouin, who has transformed the bar at the Hôtel Plaza Athénée into a hot nightspot with a cool idea: an 'iceberg' counter. The signature drink is the Rose Royale (champagne with raspberry purée). ⓐ 25 avenue Montaigne ⓣ 01 53 67 66 65 ⓦ www.plaza-athenee-paris.com ⓛ 18.00–02.00 Ⓜ Metro: Alma Marceau or Franklin D Roosevelt

**Le Duc des Lombards** One of this music-loving city's best jazz clubs attracts aficionados with its big-name performers. ⓐ 42 rue des Lombards ⓣ 01 42 33 22 88 Ⓜ Metro: Châtelet

**Rex Club** In the *hype attitude* category, this popular club is great for hardcore dancers who like shaking to house, techno and electro. ⓐ 5 boulevard Poissonnière ⓣ 01 42 36 10 96 ⓦ www.rexclub.com ⓛ 23.30–06.00 Ⓜ Metro: Bonne Nouvelle

# Right Bank East

The Right Bank East is the oldest part of Paris, including Île-de-la-Cité, Île Saint-Louis and the Marais. Much of it was untouched by the great modernisation of the 1860s, so here you still find ancient cobbled streets, small courtyards and medieval buildings that appear to sag and lean into the street. Its 10th, 19th and 20th *arrondissements* are called 'the people's Paris', while the Marais and the Bastille are hip; Bastille, particularly, hums with bars and clubs. The main attractions include the Notre-Dame cathedral, the Marais district, Canal St-Martin, the Bastille area with its modern opera house, and Père-Lachaise cemetery.

## SIGHTS & ATTRACTIONS

### Bastille

The column in the centre of the Place de la Bastille, topped by a golden liberty statue, is the symbol of the French Revolution. It was here, in 1789, that the people of Paris stormed the Bastille prison, freeing the prisoners and rising in arms against the excesses of the aristocrats and the royalty. The 51.5-m (nearly 170-ft) Colonne de Juillet commemorates the victims of two subsequent uprisings (in 1830 and 1848), who are buried in the crypt. People still rally here today during major demonstrations. The metro station's brightly-painted tiles depict scenes from the uprisings.

Today, the Bastille district in the 11th is a lively people place, with the modern Opéra Bastille and the streets surrounding the square providing a party atmosphere, especially at night and on weekends. Among the trendy clubs off the square is OPA (see 'After Dark' pages 94–7).
Ⓝ Metro: Bastille

## Paris Right Bank East

0       500 metres
0       500 yards

Barbès
Rochechouart
BOULEVARD DE ROCHOUART
La Chapelle
Stalingrad
Musée de la Musique
AVENUE JEAN-JAURÈS
Parc de la Villette & Cité des Sciences
RUE DE LA CHAPELLE
RUE LOUIS BLANC
RUE DE L'AQUEDUC
RUE D'AUBERVILLIERS
Louis Blanc
Jaurès
CITÉ LEPAGE
BOULEVARD DE MAGENTA
Gare du Nord
Gare du Nord
10e
Château Landon
RUE LA FAYETTE
RUE DU FAUBOURG SAINT DENIS
RUE DE MAUBEUGE
Gare de l'Est
Gare de l'Est
RUE LOUIS BLANC
RUE LA FAYETTE
RUE EUGÈNE VARLIN
RUE DU CHÂTEAU LANDON
RUE LOUIS BLANC
Bolivar
Buttes Chaumont
Parc des Buttes Chaumont
RUE DU PLATEAU
RUE MANIN
RUE DE CRIMÉE
RUE FESSART
RUE DE POISSONNIÈRE
RUE D'HAUTEVILLE
RUE DE CHABROL
Poissonnière
Square Villemin
QUAI DE JEMMAPES
QUAI DE VALMY
RUE DE LANCRY
QUAI DE VALMY
RUE DES VINAIGRIERS
RUE DE LA GRANGE AUX BELLES
AVENUE MATHURIN MOREAU
Colonel Fabien
Colonel Fabien
RUE SIMON BOLIVAR
AVENUE SIMON BOLIVAR
RUE DE MEAUX
RUE DE CRIMÉE
RUE PRADIER
RUE DE LA VILLETTE
RUE CLAVEL
RUE REBEVAL
Pyrénées
RUE DES PYRÉNÉES
BOULEVARD DE STRASBOURG
BOULEVARD DE MAGENTA
RUE DU FAUBOURG SAINT MARTIN
Hôtel du Nord
RUE ALIBERT
RUE BICHAT
RUE DE LA GRANGE AUX BELLES
BOULEVARD DE LA VILLETTE
Belleville
RUE RAMPONEAU
RUE DE BELLEVILLE
RUE PIAT
Strasbourg Saint Denis
RUE RENÉ BOULANGER
Chez Prune
Jacques Bonsergent
RUE DE LANCRY
Goncourt
RUE DE LA FONTAINE AU ROI
RUE SAINT MAUR
RUE DE L'ORILLON
RUE DE BELLEVILLE
Couronnes
Belleville
Parc de Belleville
BLVD SAINT MARTIN
RUE MESLAY
RUE DU VERTBOIS
PLACE DE LA RÉPUBLIQUE
BLVD DU TEMPLE
AVENUE DE LA RÉPUBLIQUE
RUE DU FAUBOURG DU TEMPLE
RUE DE LA FONTAINE AU ROI
RUE DES TROIS BORNES
BLVD DE BELLEVILLE
RUE DES COURONNES
RUE JULIEN LACROIX
RÉAUMUR SÉBASTOPOL
Musée des Arts et Métiers
Temple
Arts et Métiers
République
Oberkampf
Parmentier
RUE DU CHEMIN VERT
Ménilmontant
BOULEVARD DE SÉBASTOPOL
RUE RÉAUMUR
3e
RUE DES ARCHIVES
RUE DE TURENNE
Filles du Calvaire
RUE AMELOT
RUE JEAN-PIERRE TIMBAUD
AVENUE DE LA RÉPUBLIQUE
RUE OBERKAMPF
RUE DE CRUSSOL
RUE SAINT MAUR
Institut de Management Europe-Paris
RUE DES BLUETS
Cimitière du Père-Lachaise
RUE SAINT AMBROISE
RUE CHEMIN VERT
Arts et Métiers
RUE BEAUBOURG
RUE CHAPON
RUE RAMBUTEAU
Musée de la Poupée
Musée d'Art et d'Histoire du Judaïsme
Musée de la Chasse et de la Nature
Musée de l'Histoire de France
Musée Picasso
PGE SAINT PIERRE AMELOT
St Sébastien Froissart
Richard Lenoir
RUE RICHARD LENOIR
Marché de la Création (Bastille)
RUE SAINT SÉBASTIEN
RUE DU CHEMIN VERT
St Ambroise
BOULEVARD VOLTAIRE
BOULEVARD RICHARD LENOIR
RUE SAINT MAUR
Centre Pompidou
PIAZZA BEAUBOURG
BOULEVARD
RUE DU TEMPLE
RUE DES ARCHIVES
MARAIS
RUE DE TURENNE
RUE SAINT GILLES
BOULEVARD BEAUMARCHAIS
RUE SAINT CLAUDE
Bréguet Sabin
RUE SEDAINE
RUE DE LA ROQUETTE
RUE POPINCOURT
RUE BASFROI
RUE DE LA ROQUETTE
Voltaire
RUE DE LA ROQUETTE
Voltaire
11e
RUE KELLER
RUE DE CHARONNE
Hôtel de Ville
Hôtel de Ville
Hôtel de Ville
RUE FRANÇOIS MIRON
RUE SAINT ANTOINE
RUE DE RIVOLI
Maison Européenne de la Photographie
RUE DE SÉVIGNÉ
RUE DES FRANCS BOURGEOIS
PLACE DES VOSGES
RUE DE BIRAGUE
Maison de Victor Hugo
RUE SAINT PAUL
St Paul
RUE DE TURENNE
BOULEVARD HENRI IV
PLACE DE LA BASTILLE
Bastille
RUE DE LAPPE
AVENUE LEDRU ROLLIN
RUE DE CHARONNE
RUE BASFROI
QUAI DE L'HÔTEL DE VILLE
QUAI DES CÉLESTINS
Pont Marie
Pont Marie
QUAI DE BÉTHUNE
QUAI D'ANJOU
RUE SAINT LOUIS EN L'ÎLE
Notre-Dame
Flower & Bird Market
QUAI AUX FLEURS
QUAI DE L'ORLÉANS
QUAI DE LA TOURNELLE
Sully Morland
PONT DE SULLY
BOULEVARD HENRI IV
Bastille
Opéra Bastille
Ledru Rollin
RUE DU FAUBOURG ST ANTOINE
AVENUE LEDRU ROLLIN
RUE DE CHARENTON
RUE DE PRAGUE
RUE JULES CÉSAR
RUE CRILLON
PONT DE TOURNELLE
RUE DES FOSSÉS SAINT BERNARD
Institut du Monde Arabe
Préfecture de Paris
QUAI HENRI IV
BOULEVARD MORLAND
BOULEVARD BOURDON
RUE DE LYON
Gare de Lyon
RUE DE BERCY
RUE DE RAMBOUILLET
RUE DE CHALON
Cardinal Lemoine
Universités Paris VI Pierre et Marie
Jussieu
RUE DU CARDINAL LEMOINE
RUE CUVIER
RUE JUSSIEU
Jardin des Plantes
QUAI SAINT BERNARD
Seine
QUAI DE LA RAPÉE
Quai de la Rapée
Cinémathèque Française
Bercy Village
BOULEVARD
DIDEROT
AVENUE DAUMESNIL
RUE DE BERCY
RUE DE CHARENTON
RUE DE CITEAUX

### Legend

Ⓜ Metro Stop
✝ Cathedral
ℹ Information
⊗ Police Station
✈ Airport
🚉 Railway Stn
✚ Hospital

## Canal Cruise

A different way to look at Paris is from a canal boat. The leisurely, two-and-a-half-hour cruise on the Canal St-Martin passes through numerous locks, under footbridges and along a 595-m (650-yd) vault of the Bastille, with the Japanese artist Keiichi Tahara's 'Sounds of Light' laser light show dancing along the tunnel walls. The day-long

🔺 *View from a canal*

tour to the Marne River goes to the 'land of *guinguettes*' (riverside open-air dance clubs) and rural France. Canauxrama runs tours most days through the summer, but check with the company for a current schedule. Tours start from the Bastille's Port de l'Arsenal, a giant marina accommodating 200 boats, near the Bastille metro station.

Ⓐ Bassin de la Villette, 13 quai de la Loire Ⓣ 01 42 39 15 00
Ⓦ www.canauxrama.com Ⓜ Metro: Bastille

## Canal St-Martin

With walkable quays on both sides, Canal St-Martin is a pleasant waterway meandering from Paris-Arsenal port to La Villette basin. Barges and cruise boats can navigate using its system of nine locks. Strollers, cyclists, fishermen and roller-bladers enjoy this attractive promenade, whose Valmy and Jemmapes quays have become popular in recent years for their little boutiques, bistros and cafés. The Hôtel du Nord (Ⓐ 102 quai de Jemmapes Ⓣ 01 40 40 78 78 Ⓦ www.hoteldunord.org Ⓛ 10.00–02.00), where the film of the same name was filmed, is now a pleasant, low-key restaurant and bar.

Ⓜ Metro: République

## Cimetière du Père-Lachaise

Paris's first secular cemetery is now one of its most visited sights. Among the famous figures buried here are Molière, Apollinaire, Chopin, Modigliani, Proust and Oscar Wilde. Jim Morrison fans flock to his tomb in a never-ending pilgrimage. Fans of a different sort also visit the cemetery; an elaborate life-sized reclining bronze statue of playboy journalist Victor Noir, shot in a duel on 10 January, 1870, has become a fertility symbol, his prominent tumescence

polished to a bright shine by generations of hopeful women. With its tree-lined alleys and flowers, the Père-Lachaise is like a garden, with 44 hectares (109 acres) of greenery amid the marble, elaborate statuary and stone tombs. Neighbouring newspaper kiosks sell maps of the cemetery, which mark the famous gravestones. There are also maps posted within the grounds. The Mairie de Paris (🕿 01 42 76 47 12) conducts guided visits in English in July and August.
🅐 16 rue du Repos 🕿 08 92 68 30 00 Ⓝ Metro: Père-Lachaise

### Île Saint-Louis

Right behind Notre-Dame, Île Saint-Louis is actually made up of two islets that joined together in 1614. Laundry women once worked here, but now only the quayside façades remain, and rue Saint-Louis-en-l'Île evokes that earlier era. Below, on hot summer days sunbathers stretch out and impromptu parties break out. On the opposite banks, *bouquinistes* sell their second-hand books, postcards and posters. The sounds of African and Latin American drumming is often heard along the quays, along with tour-boat commentary in many languages.
Ⓝ Metro: Saint-Paul

### Maison de Victor Hugo

You've read the books or seen the movies: *Les Misérables*, *The Hunchback of Notre Dame*, *Notre-Dame de Paris*. Now you can see where the poet, novelist and playwright Victor Hugo lived. The author's house looks over the historic red-brick Place des Vosges, a fashionable residence in its day. Permanent collections have free admission.
🅐 6 Place des Vosges 🕿 01 42 72 10 16 🕘 10.00–18.00, closed Mon
Ⓝ Metro: République

## Marais

One of the city's oldest areas, the Marais (a marsh drained to make aristocrats' mansions in the 16th century) is an intimate area of specialty boutiques, restaurants and museums. The district is great for strolling, with its narrow streets, ancient timbered house, cobbled cloisters, a mosaic-covered building, fountains, squares, surprising architectural details and buildings so aged they lean into the street. Many Marais shops, particularly on rue Francs Bourgeois, are open on Sunday.

## Notre-Dame

With its dusky white towers rising above the Île-de-la-Cité in the centre of the Seine, the Notre-Dame cathedral, a Gothic masterpiece, is one of the best-loved sights of Paris. Victor Hugo immortalised the cathedral in his novel *The Hunchback of Notre-Dame*. The French version of the film of the same name (1957) has wonderful scenes of the hunchback (played by Anthony Quinn) and the gypsy Esmeralda on the balcony of the towers, with jutting gargoyles and views of Paris. Tower visits are free on the first Sunday of the month.

Often unnoticed, a brass plaque in the stones of the parvis (square) in front of the Notre-Dame marks kilometer zero. Distances to various destinations in France are marked from that point.

Directly in front of the cathedral, and overlooked by many sightseers, a staircase leads down to the archeological **Crypt** of the Parvis of Notre-Dame, housing vestiges of earlier civilisations, from Gallo-Roman to the 19th century. They were first discovered during excavations in the 1960s. The largest structure of its type in the world, it extends 118 m (387 ft).

**Cathedral** ⓐ 6 Parvis-de-Notre-Dame, Île-de-la-Cité ⓣ 01 53 10 07 00
ⓦ www.monum.fr & www.cathedraledeparis.com ⓛ tower
10.00–17.30 Oct–Mar, 09.30–19.30 Apr–June & Sept, 09.00–19.30
July–Aug; cathedral 08.00–18.45 Mon–Sat, 08.00–19.45 Sun
ⓜ Metro: St-Michel or Cité
**Crypt** ⓐ 6 Place du Parvis-de-Notre-Dame, Île-de-la-Cité ⓣ 01 42 34
56 10 ⓦ www.cathedraledeparis.com ⓛ 10.00–18.00, closed Mon
ⓜ Metro: Cité

### Opéra Bastille

Designed by Carlos Ott and opened in 1989 for the bicentenary of
the French Revolution, the curved, glass-faced Opéra Bastille has
transformed the face of the Bastille district. A full programme of
opera and dance is available throughout the year (except August).
The building is known for its excellent acoustics – all the better to
hear the singers' *bel canto*.
ⓐ Place de la Bastille ⓣ 01 40 01 19 70 ⓦ www.opera-de-paris.fr
ⓜ Metro: Bastille

### Parc de la Villette

Park, concert venue, cultural complex, La Villette is all these rolled
into one lively, entertaining destination. The 28-hectare (69-acre)
urban park has everything from bamboo grove to sprawling lawns
where the open-air cinema festival is held in summer. In the
spherical Géode, a huge, hemispheric screen shows compelling
documentaries often on nature and the planet. La Villette also
includes the Cité des Sciences and the Musée de la Musique (see
'Culture' opposite).
ⓣ 01 40 03 75 75 ⓦ www.villette.com ⓜ Metro: Porte de la Villette

### Place de la République

Along with the Bastille, the Place de la République is known as a people and party place. A giant bronze statue representing the French Republic stands at its centre.

Ⓜ Metro: République

## CULTURE

### Centre Pompidou

Whatever you may think of the industrial chic look, this is France's most important modern art museum, with such major expositions as Dada and 'Los Angeles'. You can see great views from its top floor and the Georges restaurant. On the first Sunday of the month admission to the exhibitions is free. The Piazza Beaubourg in front of the Centre Pompidou is an animated gathering place, with musicians and other performers amusing the crowds, so you can enjoy this destination even if you don't wish to art-gaze.

ⓐ Place Georges Pompidou ☏ 01 44 78 12 33

Ⓦ www.centrepompidou.fr ⏱ 11.00–21.00 Wed–Mon

Ⓜ Metro: Rambuteau

### Cité des Sciences

Part of the Parc de la Villette, the Cité des Sciences always has some interesting exhibit connected with inventions and human behaviour. Interactive exhibits cover Earth matters from volcanoes to oceans. There is also a planetarium and 3-D cinema.

ⓐ 30 avenue Corentin-Cariou ☏ 01 40 05 80 00

Ⓦ www.cite-sciences.fr ⏱ 10.00–18.00 (until 19.00 Sun), closed Mon

Ⓜ Metro: Porte de la Villette

> **FLAMING FILM**
> In the 1930s, film was almost worthless, and resold by weight for recycling. Miles of film rotted away in cellars, occasionally bursting into flame.

### La Cinémathèque Française
This museum of film reopened in the Bercy area of Paris in 2005. The treasure trove of movie history includes an exceptional collection of 40,000 films plus a documentation centre, exhibition halls and four movie theatres showing classic films from all types of cinema year-round.

ⓐ 51 rue de Bercy, Parc de Bercy ⓣ 01 71 19 33 33
ⓦ www.cinematheque.fr ⓛ 12.00–19.00 Mon, Wed & Fri, 12.00–22.00 Thur, 10.00–20.00 Sat & Sun, closed Tues
Ⓝ Metro: Bercy

### Maison Européenne de la Photographie
Dedicated to contemporary artists, this gallery holds regular exhibits of work by major contemporary photographers, displaying the three basic media of photographic art: exhibition prints, the printed page and film.

ⓐ 82 rue François Miron ⓣ 33 01 44 78 75 00 ⓛ 11.00–20.00, closed Mon & Tues Ⓝ Metro: Saint-Paul or Pont Marie

### Musée de la Musique
Featuring a 900-year history of musical instruments, the museum is part of the Cité de la Musique, which houses several concert halls, a music school and the Paris Conservatoire in the Parc de la Villette.

🅐 221 avenue Jean-Jaurés 🕿 01 44 84 45 00 🅦 www.cite-musique.fr
🕓 12.00–18.00 Tues–Sat, 10.00–18.00 Sun Ⓝ Metro: Porte de Pantin

🔺 *The eye-catching science museum*

### Musée des Arts et Métiers

This fascinating museum dedicated to inventions and technology
from the 16th century to today houses some 80,000 objects.
Exhibits include steam-powered vehicles, such as Cugnot's
Fardier, and planes flown by Louis Blériot and Clément Ader.
The building, an ancient priory, is particularly appealing. Even
the metro station is inventive, like the inside of a copper-toned
submarine. ⓐ 60 rue Réaumur ❶ 01 53 01 82 00 ⓦ www.arts-et-
metiers.net ⓛ 10.00–18.00 (until 21.30 Thur), closed Mon
ⓜ Metro: Arts et Métiers

### Musée Picasso

Located in the beautiful 17th-century Hôtel Salé (salty hotel),
this is the largest collection of Picasso's paintings, sculptures and
photographs under one roof. The museum affords a wonderful
opportunity for fans to see so many of the artist's works assembled
together, as well as his collection of paintings by Matisse, Renoir and
Cézanne, among others from 1901–63. On the first Sunday of the
month admission is free. ⓐ 5 rue de Thorigny ❶ 01 42 71 25 21
ⓦ www.musee-picasso.fr ⓛ 09.30–18.00 (summer); 09.30–17.30,
closed Tues (winter) ⓜ Metro: Saint-Paul

## RETAIL THERAPY

**Alternatives** This tiny boutique in the Marais features couture cast-
offs (mainly for men) from such designers as Gucci, Issy Miyake
and Jean-Paul Gaultier. ⓐ 18 rue du Roi-de-Sicile ❶ 01 42 78 31 50
ⓛ 13.00–18.30 Tues–Sat ⓜ Metro: Saint-Paul

**Antoine & Lili** Local clothing designers have created a hit line of reasonably priced clothes and accessories for women in Antoine & Lili. Stores in bright pinks, yellows and greens are cheerful and fun. Several locations around Paris. ⓐ 95 quai de Valmy & 51 rue de Francs Bourgeois ⓣ 01 42 05 62 23 ⓦ www.antoineetlili.com ⓝ Metro: République or Hôtel de Ville

**Bercy Village** Shopping, dining and relaxing in a riverside atmosphere are all here at the Cour Saint-Emilion in Bercy Village. This is not just a commercial venture. People live in this engaging complex that was once the world's largest wine market. There is even a bakery school. Club Med runs restaurants and a nightclub here (see 'After Dark' pages 94–7). ⓣ 01 40 02 90 80 ⓦ www.bercyvillage.com ⓝ Metro: Bercy

**Concept Nature** A conveniently located African shop with decorative items from Togo, Ghana, Mali, Congo and Kenya, Concept Nature features gift and household items, including candleholders, lamps, carved chairs and bowls and traditional African instruments. ⓐ 28 rue de Rivoli ⓣ 01 42 77 11 19 ⓝ Metro: Saint-Paul

**CSAO** The spacious Compagnie de Senegal et de l'Afrique de l'Ouest reflects Paris's rich African population, promoting the best of Senegal in this cheerful shop with its 'sustainably minded' accessories and trinkets. Bright little plastic bracelets resembling beaded bangles are a modern version of the old elephant hair bracelets Senegalese ladies wore. Rhythmic African CDs, paintings, baskets aplenty, funky furniture from recycled materials and calabash gourd bowls are all sold. ⓐ 1–3 rue Elzévir ⓣ 01 44 54 55 88 ⓛ 11.00–19.00 Mon–Sat, 14.00–19.00 Sun ⓝ Metro: Saint-Paul

**Flower & Bird Market** The flower market is a sight to behold with its array of colourful and aromatic flora. On Sundays, songbirds, cockatoos and other feathered friends are also sold here. ⓐ Place Louis-Lepine, Île-de-la-Cité 🕐 bird market 09.00–19.00 Sun, flower market 08.00–19.00 Ⓝ Metro: La Cité

🔺 *Try shopping for women's clothes here*

**Marché de la Création** Vendors at Bastille's outdoor market display a wide variety of arts, crafts and also junk. ⓐ boulevard Richard Lenoir ⓦ www.marchecreation.com ⓛ 09.00–18.00 Sat ⓝ Metro: Bastille

**Viaduc des Arts** A renovated train viaduct has metamorphosed into a clutch of craftsmen's shops and showrooms at the Viaduc des Arts. Above is as delightful a surprise as the brick boutiques below. Here, the elevated Promenade Plantée, a flowering footpath linking several gardens, winds nearly 5 km (3 miles) along an old railway line to the Bois de Vincennes. The peaceful urban 'lung' provides a great, unobstructed view of the 12th *arrondissement*. ⓝ Metro: Bastille

## TAKING A BREAK

**L'Apparement Café £ ❶** In this cosy café in the Marais near the Picasso museum, patrons play chess and relax. Sunday is *journée brunch*. ⓐ 18 rue des Coutures Saint-Gervais ⓣ 01 48 87 12 22 ⓛ 12.00–02.00 (from 12.30 Sun) ⓝ Metro: St-Sebastien Froissart

**Berthillon £ ❷** Even on rainy, cold days there is a queue at Berthillon, the city's finest ice-cream shop, which has been preparing its tasty products in a small factory behind the boutique on Île Saint-Louis since the mid-1950s. Choose from more than 20 exotic flavours. ⓐ 29–31 rue Saint-Louis-en-l'Île ⓣ 01 43 54 31 61 ⓦ www.berthillon.fr ⓛ 10.00–20.00, closed Mon & Tues ⓝ Metro: Pont Marie

**Chez Prune £ ❸** A cheerful little bar/restaurant with mango-yellow walls and a slightly worn look. Staff are very friendly and

there's a lively buzz. ⓐ 71 quai du Valmy ⓣ 01 42 41 30 47
🕐 08.00–01.45 Ⓜ Metro: Goncourt

**Finkelsztajn's £** ❹ The sign on Sacha Finkelsztajn's window reads
'Gastronomie Europe Centrale et Russie'. Polish immigrants founded
the original store on this colourful Jewish street in 1851, and now
two family-owned shops (Florence Finkelsztajn a few doors down)
sell such specialties as cheesecake, poppy seed, fig or date cakes,
huge cinnamon-sprinkled apple strudels and golden loaves of
just-baked bread. Deli items include traditional sausages, dill pickles
and salads.
**Florence** ⓐ 24 rue des Ecouffes ⓣ 01 48 87 92 85 🕐 10.00–19.00,
closed Wed Ⓜ Metro: Saint-Paul
**Sacha** ⓐ 27 rue des Rosiers ⓣ 01 42 72 78 91 🕐 10.00–19.00
Wed–Mon (from 11.00 Mon) Ⓜ Metro: Saint-Paul

## AFTER DARK

### Restaurants
**Bistro Marguerite £** ❺ This Seine-side gem, with its view of the
Hôtel de Ville and riverside setting, is a typical French bistro with a
rustic, country décor, friendly staff and reasonable prices. Choices
include such traditional French fare as *aligot* (puréed cheese and
garlic potatoes) and tender pork knuckle. Also open for breakfast
and lunch. ⓐ 2 quai de Gesvres ⓣ 01 42 72 00 04 Ⓜ Metro: Hôtel
de Ville

**Hermes et Bacchus £** ❻ An unpretentious wine bar near the Gare
de Lyon, as popular with the locals as it is with tourists. Traditional
fare with menu changing daily, according to market availability.

ⓐ 6 rue Emile-Gilbert ⓣ 01 40 01 91 80 ⓛ lunch & dinner, closed Sun
ⓜ Metro: Gare de Lyon

**La Tartine £ ❼**   Paris's oldest wine bar attracts a young clientele.
It is also one of the friendliest and most reasonably priced. Amid
an Art Deco décor, the restaurant serves *tartines* (sandwiches)
and meals a cut above the standard steak-and-chips bistro fare.
ⓐ 24 rue de Rivoli ⓣ 01 42 72 76 85 ⓛ 08.00–02.00 ⓜ Metro:
Saint-Paul

**Le Coude Fou £–££ ❽**   With its naïve paintings on the walls and
ceiling, the quirky 'Crazy Elbow' wine bar/restaurant serves good,
typically French food with a wide choice of wines. ⓐ 2 rue du Bourg-
Tibourg ⓣ 01 42 77 15 16 ⓛ 12.00–15.00 & 19.30–02.00 ⓜ Metro:
Hôtel de Ville

**Café de l'Industrie ££ ❾**   Serving customers in the Bastille area
for some 17 years, this restaurant attracts a youthful crowd for its
good food at reasonable prices. Lamb *noisettes* and fresh fish are
typical menu items. Staff are young and enthusiastic and décor is
'anthropological', with old colonial outpost photos, masks and fan
palms. Two locations. ⓐ 16 & 17 rue Saint Sabin ⓣ 01 47 00 13 53
ⓛ 10.00–02.00 ⓜ Metro: Bastille

**La Tête Ailleurs ££ ❿**   In an old building in the Marais, this
restaurant has been gentrified to provide a warm, Provençal
farmhouse atmosphere. The food is excellent and the service
friendly, but not fawning. ⓐ 20 rue Beautreillis ⓣ 01 42 72 47 80
ⓦ www.lateteailleurs-restaurant-paris.com ⓛ 12.00–14.00 &
20.00–22.30 Mon–Fri, 20.00–22.30 Sat ⓜ Metro: Saint-Paul

**Le Train Bleu ££ (set menu) £££ (à la carte)** ⓫ With its Belle Epoque ceiling hung with chandeliers and painted with scenes of Paris and other cities, this grand restaurant and its Big Ben Bar evoke an earlier, less-hurried age. Situated above the Gare de Lyon, which was built for the 1900 World Fair, the dining room is the best-preserved part of the original building. Its wonderful paintings were recently restored to their original state. The restaurant attracts a mixed clientele: young locals, travellers and older Parisians who long for a quiet, genteel atmosphere. As its brochure says, outside in the modern world, 'linear design has triumphed over the curves of Baroque art'. Even if you don't wish to have a drink or a meal, it is worth popping your head in to catch a glimpse of this splendid setting. ⓐ Gare de Lyon ⓣ 01 43 43 09 06 ⓦ www.le-train-bleu.com ⓜ Metro: Gare de Lyon

### Bars, clubs & entertainment

**Bercy** Live concerts are held just about every night here, with a whole range of music, including jazz, rock, hip-hop and rhythm-and-blues. ⓐ 12 boulevard du Bercy ⓣ 01 40 02 60 60 ⓦ www.bercy.fr ⓜ Metro: Bercy

**Club Med World** A complex run by the famous French resort group, which includes two restaurants and two bars/discothèques. ⓐ 39 cour St-Emilion, Bercy ⓣ 08 10 81 04 10 ⓦ www.clubmedworld.fr ⓛ 11.00–02.00 Tues–Thur, 11.00–06.00 Fri & Sat, 11.00–08.00 Sun ⓜ Metro: Bercy

**Flèche d'Or Café** This cavernous space, in a former train station, is popular for its live bands. Music ranges from Afro and reggae to rock, jazz and rhythm-and-blues, among other genres. You have to

queue to get in, and you take your chances with the music, which
can be great reggae or high-volume, amateurish ear abuse. ❷ 102
bis rue de Bagnolet ❶ 01 44 64 01 02 ⓦ www.flechedor.com
ⓝ Metro: Porte de Bagnolet

**La Fontaine** For an evening of excellent jazz, locals say it is hard to
beat La Fontaine. ❷ 20 rue de la Grange aux Belles ❶ 01 42 45 36 27
❶ from 21.30 ⓝ Metro: Colonel Fabien

**New Morning** A former printing shop, this Paris institution is known
for its concerts of jazz and world music. ❷ 7–9 rue des Petites-
Ecuries ❶ 01 45 23 51 41 ⓦ www.newmorning.com ❶ 20.00–01.30
Mon–Sat ⓝ Metro: Château d'Eau

**OPA** This nightclub is a good deal in the Bastille, with free entry to
live music, electro, rock and other sounds. ❷ 9 rue Biscornet ❶ 01 46
28 12 90 ⓦ www.opa-paris.com ❶ 20.00–06.00 many nights
ⓝ Metro: Bastille

### Night views
All of the Seine's bridges are illuminated at night, so anywhere you
walk along the river you get that quintessential romantic Paris
perspective. Diners at the Bistro Marguerite (see page 94) get
splendid night views of the Seine right across the street, and
perhaps the moon lighting the scene from above. Across the Place
de l'Hôtel de Ville, the grand town hall is spotlit at night and glows
beside the Seine.

# Left Bank

The Left Bank is the Paris of universities and bohemia, of literary cafés, student hangouts and artists' ateliers and galleries. Such historically important buildings as the Sorbonne, the Panthéon, the Eiffel Tower and the Musée d'Orsay are all found here. Although they are located on islands in the Seine, Notre-Dame and the Conciergerie are actually in the 1st *arrondissement*, and so are listed under the Right Bank. Called the Rive Gauche in French, the large and varied Left Bank of Paris includes the legendary Latin Quarter in the 5th *arrondissement*, the more bourgeois 7th, where the Eiffel Tower and Invalides stand, and the soaring Tour Montparnasse in the 15th.

## SIGHTS & ATTRACTIONS

### Boulevard Saint-Germain
While the Champs-Elysées is the grand thoroughfare of the Right Bank, Saint-Germain is the main boulevard of the Left, where boutiques and bistros, cafés and cinemas, street entertainers and *flâneurs* (strollers) all converge. It is also known for its little jazz joints and art galleries on side streets such as rue de Seine, rue des Beaux-Arts and rue Bonaparte.

### Eglise Saint-Sulpice
This fine church is noted for its paintings by Eugène Delacroix (first chapel on the right as you enter) and for its organ, circa 1862, which is famous throughout Europe. The fountain square in front is a popular place to rest.
ⓐ Place Saint-Sulpice ⓞ 01 46 33 21 78 ⓞ 08.00–19.30 ⓝ Metro: Saint-Sulpice

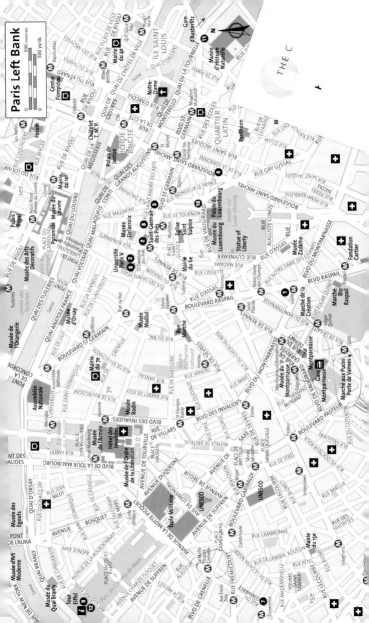

# Paris Left Bank

500 meters
500 yards

## ôtel des Invalides

Recognisable for its gold-leaf dome shining brilliantly along the Left Bank horizon, the Hôtel des Invalides is where Napoleon is buried. Indeed, he got the royal-internment treatment. His ashes are protected in a sarcophagus containing six coffins, of iron, lead and wood. One of the most beautiful 17th-century monuments of Paris, Les Invalides was built during the time of Louis XIV to house wounded soldiers. Parts of it are still used as a hospital. There are five museums here, including the Musée de l'Armée. Its Cathédrale Saint-Louis occasionally has classical music concerts.

ⓐ esplanade des Invalides ⓦ www.invalides.org ⓛ 10.00–18.00 (summer); 10.00–17.00 (winter) Ⓜ Metro: Invalides

## Jardin des Plantes

Part of the natural history museum (see 'Culture' pages 107–12) and dating back to a 17th-century garden of medicinal plants, the Jardin des Plantes has one of the most beautiful rose gardens in Paris, with some 350 varieties. There are also alpine and tropical gardens, the garden's roots, medicinal plants, as well as a micro-zoo and menagerie.

ⓐ entrance on rue Cuvier ⓛ 09.00–18.00 (summer); 09.00–17.00, closed Tues (winter) Ⓜ Metro: Jussieu

## Jardin du Luxembourg

Adjacent to the Senate building, this is a true Parisian park, with an orderly French garden, tree-lined alleys, green spaces, statuary and *bassins* (ponds) around which Parisians sit on fine days. The *guignol* (a Punch and Judy type puppet theatre) still entertains children as it has done for centuries. You can watch regulars playing *boules*, bridge

● *The beautiful Jardin des Plantes is worth a visit*

and chess, or just hang around like the locals, lounging on the metal chairs watching children sail miniature boats in the ornamental pond. A hidden charm in the west side of the Jardin du Luxembourg is the bronze model of the Statue of Liberty, which the sculptor Auguste Bartholdi gave to the garden in 1900 for the World Fair. Bartholdi, who sculpted the full-sized Statue of Liberty that now stands in New York harbour, based his masterpiece on this model and a larger one that fronts the Pont de Grenelle in the Seine.

🄰 rue de Vaugirard 🄻 sunrise–sunset 🄽 RER B: Luxembourg

### Latin Quarter

So-named because the students and teachers of the Sorbonne spoke Latin until the French Revolution (1789), the Latin Quarter in the 5th *arrondissement* has long been associated with students, writers and intellectuals. While it is still abuzz with universities and young intellectuals, it has expanded beyond a centre of learning to become a *quartier* of cafés and bars, boutiques, bistros and nightspots. The area includes the lively Saint-Michel warren of cobbled streets and restaurants, the Sorbonne, the Panthéon and the medieval Cluny museum. Bustling and narrow, rue Mouffetard is one of the city's oldest streets; it was the main road from Paris (then called Lutèce) to Rome in ancient times. 'Le Mouff' has a lively weekend market, little boutiques and reasonably priced restaurants. There is even a Roman arena, the Arènes de Lutèce. In this admission-free Gallo-Roman ruin, which was once a circus amphitheatre, young boys kick footballs around, while couples seek a quiet corner.

**Arènes de Lutèce** 🄰 47 rue Monge 🄻 08.00–22.00 (summer); 08.00–17.30 (winter) 🄽 Metro: Cardinal-Lemoine

## Markets

Paris's markets are an attraction in themselves, reminiscent of the traditional form of country commerce, where vendors call out their wares to passersby and goods range from fresh, tempting foodstuffs to books, birds and collectables.

**Marché Bio Raspail** Organic food market. boulevard Raspail 08.30–13.30 Sun Metro: Sèvres-Babylone

**Marché Couvert Monge** At this covered food market in the Latin Quarter, vocal vendors sell a wide range of produce, meat, cheese and delicacies. Place Monge 08.30–13.30 Wed, Fri & Sun Metro: Place Monge

**Marché Parisien de la Création** At this outdoor arts and crafts market, painters, sculptors, ceramicists and other artisans sell their wares directly to the public. near the Gare Montparnasse, at the foot of the Tour Montparnasse 01 53 57 42 63 www.marchecreation.com 09.00–18.00 Sun Metro: Edgar Quinet

**Marché aux Puces de la Porte de Vanves** Past the polyester clothing stalls and oddball junk, you can find some gems at this flea market, such as lace fabrics, antique tables and silverware. Avenue Georges Lafenestre & avenue Marc Saugnier 06 86 89 99 96 www.pucesdeparis-portedevanves.com 09.00–19.00 Sat & Sun Metro: Porte de Vanves

## Odéon

The Odéon district of boulevard Saint-Germain is always abuzz with students, shoppers and movie-goers (there are several major cinema complexes here). Shops range from couture to little boutiques and there are also theatres, bookstores and cafés, including Paris's oldest café, Le Procope (see page 115).
Metro: Odéon

## Panthéon

One of the most recognised of Paris monuments is the Panthéon, in the 5th *arrondissement*. Since 1791, this stately, domed structure has been the revered resting place of some of France's most eminent figures, including Voltaire, Victor Hugo, Jean-Jacques Rousseau, Emile Zola, Marie Curie and a recent inductee, Alexander Dumas. Tours of the nave and crypt are available. A fascinating permanent exhibit is that of Foucault's pendulum, which hangs from high above in the dome's crown and swings slowly and hypnotically by observers near the Panthéon floor, demonstrating that the earth really does move for you.

ⓐ Place du Panthéon ⓣ for guided visits 01 44 13 18 00
ⓦ www.monum.fr ⓛ 10.00–18.30 (summer); 10.00–18.15 (winter)
ⓝ Metro: Cardinal Lemoine

## Saint-Germain-des-Prés

This Romanesque church on the boulevard bearing its name has the oldest belfry in Paris. Inside it is very peaceful, a wonderful place to ponder. On the corner of the boulevard Saint-Germain-des-Prés are the legendary literary cafés Les Deux Magots and Café Flore (see page 113).

ⓝ Metro: Saint-Germain-des-Prés

## Seine

The city was first settled on an island (the Île-de-la-Cité) on the Seine, and the river remains one of its most appealing and vital features. Many of the city's finest attractions are found along its banks: the Louvre, Musée d'Orsay, the Eiffel Tower, Notre-Dame and the Conciergerie. The Seine can be appreciated on a stroll along its quays

ⓞ *Ornate gold statues adorn the Pont Alexander*

with its 37 distinctive bridges, or from one of the many cruise boats. Especially romantic are night-time dinner cruises.

**Bâteaux Parisiens** depart from the foot of the Eiffel Tower hourly from 10.00 to 23.00 (until 22.00 in winter). Lunch and dinner cruises are also available. ☎ 01 46 99 43 13 🌐 www.bateauxparisiens.com

**Batobus**, a regular boat service making eight stops along the Seine, is like an inexpensive cruise, without the commentary. Service operates year-round except January and gives a great tranquil perspective of some of Paris's most famous buildings. ☎ 08 25 05 01 01 🌐 www.batobus.com

### Tour Eiffel (Eiffel Tower)

Gustave Eiffel built the most visible and well-known site of Paris and the symbol of France worldwide, the graceful Tour Eiffel, for the 1889 World Fair. When it was first assembled, the tower was widely disparaged. Parisians called it a pitiful lamppost and a hollow candlestick. Today, the French, and visitors from around the world, admire the filigreed, A-shaped structure above the Seine. At 324 m high (1,063 ft), the tower has 1,665 steps and requires some 50 tonnes of paint to repaint it in 'Tour Eiffel Brown'. 20,000 light bulbs light it like a birthday sparkler each hour after dark until 01.00. There are lifts to the three levels, which cost more the higher you go. Staircases to levels one and two are open only till 18.00.

ⓐ Champs-de-Mars ☎ 01 44 11 23 23 🌐 www.tour.eiffel.fr
🕐 09.30–23.00 (last lift for the top 22.30); 09.00–24.00 mid-June–end Aug Ⓜ Metro: Bir-Hakeim

### Tour Montparnasse

Although it is a black blight on the Paris skyline, the Tour Montparnasse redeems itself through its spectacular view from the 56th floor. With its 210-m (689-ft) terrace and café, the highest in Paris, the views really are superb on a clear day or night, with all of Paris spread out below.

ⓐ rue de l'Arrivée ⓣ 01 45 38 52 56 ⓦ www.tourmontparnasse56.com ⓛ 09.30–23.30 Apr–Sept; 09.30–22.30 Sun–Thur, 09.30–23.00 Fri, Sat & eves of holidays, last elevator up leaves half an hour before closing ⓝ Metro: Montparnasse-Bienvenüe

## CULTURE

### Fondation Cartier

With its large, airy spaces to display its collection, the Fondation Cartier, established in 1984, is a private foundation for contemporary art. Big, glass windows let in the natural light, while outside grounds filled with tall trees emphasise the height of the display space and give a sense of bringing the outdoors in. Exhibitions focus on individual artists or themes from design to photography, painting to video.

ⓐ 261 boulevard Raspail ⓣ 01 42 18 56 50 ⓦ www.fondationcartier.com ⓛ 12.00–20.00 Tues–Sun ⓝ Metro: Raspail

### Musée Delacroix

The painter's last home and atelier is now a charming, intimate museum, with displays of his work as well as memorabilia and letters to his friends such as Charles Baudelaire and Georges Sand. Admission is free on the first Sunday of the month.

ⓐ 6 rue Furstenberg ⓣ 01 44 41 86 50 ⓦ www.musee-delacroix.fr ⓛ 09.30–17.00, closed Tues ⓝ Metro: Saint-Germain-des-Prés

## Musée des Égouts

It may sound odd, but a guided tour of the Sewer Museum of Paris provides an interesting look at the underbelly of the city.

ⓐ Pont de l'Alma (Place de la Résistance) on the corner of 93 quai d'Orsay ⓣ 01 47 05 10 29 ⓦ www.paris.fr ⓛ 11.00–17.00 (summer); 11.00–16.00, closed Thur, Fri & several weeks in Jan (winter)

ⓜ Metro: Alma-Marceau

## Musée d'Histoire Naturelle

It's Jurassic Park without the violence at this natural history museum, where you can see reconstructions of dinosaurs, African game such as giraffes, and marine species. The evolution gallery, with its extinct and threatened species, makes you think of what we need to protect and preserve. Spectacular displays throughout its galleries and gardens.

ⓐ 57 rue Cuvier ⓣ 01 40 79 56 01 ⓦ www.mnhn.fr ⓛ 09.00–18.00 (summer); 09.00–17.00, closed Tues (winter) ⓜ Metro: Jussieu

## Musée d'Orsay

More than a museum, this grand structure, built as a train station for the World Fair in 1900, is an attraction in itself. The light-filled rooms and lofty, luminous central gallery set off some of the world's greatest artworks to their best advantage. The permanent collection encompasses the whole range of fine arts from the mid-19th century to the early 20th. The upper floor is devoted to Impressionists and Post-Impressionists, with famous works by Monet, Renoir, Degas, Cézanne, Pissarro, Sisley and Van Gogh. As well as the permanent collections, there are always rotating exhibitions. In summer, the open-air terrace on Musée d'Orsay's

ⓞ *Come and admire the beautiful clock in Musée d'Orsay*

level five gives a fabulous view of the Seine and all the historic riverfront buildings. Admission to the museum is free on the first Sunday of the month.

The recently rebuilt Passerelle de Solferino pedestrian bridge across the Seine links the Musée d'Orsay in a graceful steel arch with the Jardin des Tuileries on the Right Bank.

ⓐ 1 rue de la Légion d'honneur ❶ 01 40 49 48 14
ⓦ www.musee-orsay.fr ⏱ 10.00–18.00 Tues–Sat, 10.00–21.45 Thur, 09.00–18.00 Sun & June 20–Sept 20 Ⓝ Metro: Solférino

### Musée du Luxembourg

Some of the city's most important visiting exhibitions are held in the former orangery of the Senate building in the Jardin du Luxembourg.

ⓐ 19 rue de Vaugirard ❶ 01 42 34 25 95, reservations 08 92 68 46 94
ⓦ www.museeduluxembourg.fr, reservations www.billet-coupe-file.com ⏱ 11.00–19.00 Tues, Wed & Thur, 11.00–22.00 Mon, Fri & Sat, 09.00–19.00 Sun Ⓝ RER B: Luxembourg

### Musée du Montparnasse

Visiting this museum is like stepping back in time to 19th-century painters' Paris. The entrance into this charming former painter's studio/canteen is via a peaceful cobbled alleyway.

ⓐ 21 avenue du Maine ❶ 01 42 22 91 96
ⓦ www.museedumontparnasse.net ⏱ 12.30–19.00 Tues–Sun
Ⓝ Metro: Montparnasse-Bienvenüe

### Musée du Quai Branly

This new and long-awaited museum along the Seine next to the Eiffel Tower houses arts and artefacts from civilisations of Africa, Asia, Oceania and the Americas. Among its collections are items

moved from the Musée de l'Homme and the Musée des Arts
d'Afrique et d'Océanie.

ⓐ 55 quai Branly ⓣ 01 56 61 70 00 ⓦ www.quaibranly.fr
ⓛ 10.00–18.00, closed Mon ⓜ Metro: Bir-Hakeim; RER C: Pont de
l'Alma

### Musée Maillol Fondation Dina Vierny

This museum displays works by Maillol, including sculptures and
paintings, as well as works from the private collection of Dina Vierny,
such as those by Matisse, Gauguin, Rousseau and Kandinsky. It also
holds temporary exhibitions of such well-known artists as Duffy
and Fernando Botero. The charming, barrel-vaulted café in the
basement serves drinks and snacks.

ⓐ 59–61 rue de Grenelle ⓣ 01 42 22 59 58 ⓦ www.museemaillol.com
ⓛ 11.00–18.00, closed Tues ⓜ Metro: Rue du Bac

### Musée Rodin

The Musée Rodin provides a pleasant, green escape in the heart of
Paris. Housed in a delightful, 18th-century mansion, the museum
contains bronze and marble work by Auguste Rodin (1840–1917), as
well as works by Van Gogh, Monet, Renoir and others. Famous Rodin
sculptures such as *The Thinker*, *The Kiss* and *Eve* are scattered
through the garden. The building and garden may be visited
separately.

ⓐ 79 rue de Varenne ⓣ 01 44 18 61 10 ⓦ www.musee-rodin.fr
ⓛ 09.30–16.45, closed Mon ⓜ Metro: Varenne

### Musée Zadkine

The Russian artist Ossip Zadkine (1890–1967) bequeathed his home
and garden to the city of Paris. Some 100 of his works here include

distinctive sculptures in bronze and tree trunks. After renovations,
the museum reopened in 2006.

**ⓐ** 100 bis rue d'Assas **ⓣ** 01 55 42 77 20 **ⓦ** www.paris.fr
**ⓛ** 10.00–18.00, closed Mon and public holidays **ⓝ** RER B: Port-Royal

## RETAIL THERAPY

**Debauve et Gallais** In 1800, pharmacists of Louis XVI, suppliers to
the king, founded this store. Now a famous *chocolatier*, the boutique
is like a temple of chocolate. **ⓐ** 30 rue des Saints-Pères **ⓣ** 01 45 48 54
67 **ⓦ** www.debauve-et-gallais.com **ⓛ** 09.00–19.00, closed Sun
**ⓝ** Metro: Saint-Germain-des-Prés

**La Bagagerie** These stores sell all kinds of bags, from little clutches
and practical office totes to wheeled suitcases. Prices are reasonable
and staff friendly. Several locations. **ⓐ** 41 rue du Four **ⓣ** 01 45 48 85
88 **ⓦ** www.labagagerie.com **ⓛ** 10.15–19.00 **ⓝ** Metro: Mabillon

**La Maison Ivre** This small boutique sells distinctive Provençal
ceramics with jugs, bowls, tiles and other items coloured in the
warm hues of the Mediterranean. **ⓐ** 38 rue Jacob **ⓣ** 01 42 60 01 85
**ⓦ** www.fourmi.com/maison-ivre **ⓛ** 10.30–19.00, closed Sun
**ⓝ** Metro: Saint-Germain-des-Prés

**Le Bon Marché** The oldest department store in Paris is nonetheless
*très chic*, known for its ready-to-wear items, household goods and
La Grande Epicerie (at No 38), with some 5,000 of the world's finest
foodstuffs as well as a deli. Some of the little streets around Le Bon
Marché, such as rue de l'Abbé Grégoire and rue Saint-Placide, often
have sales and low prices. **ⓐ** 24 rue de Sèvres **ⓣ** 01 44 39 80 00

Ⓦ www.lebonmarche.fr Ⓛ 09.30–19.00 Mon–Fri (until 21.00 Thur), 09.30–20.00 Sat Ⓝ Metro: Sèvres-Babylone

**Les Filles à la Vanille** With three boutiques on the Left Bank, Les Filles à la Vanille stocks clothes, accessories and bags for women. Ⓐ 1 rue de l'Ancienne Comédie (corner of Buci) Ⓣ 01 43 26 61 66 Ⓝ Metro: Odéon

**Zadig & Voltaire** Designer jeans, bags and t-shirts, some affordable, by such creators as Helmut Lang and Yoshi Nagasawa. Ⓐ 1 rue du Vieux-Colombier Ⓣ 01 43 29 18 29 Ⓝ Metro: Saint-Sulpice

## TAKING A BREAK

**La Coupole £** ❶   This famous 1900s brasserie in Montparnasse has rotating artwork displays, such as portraits of celebrated patrons of the past (like Hemingway and Jean-Paul Sartre). It is open for full meals, but for a light snack, the 'Formule Thé' (€8.50) includes a tasty pastry, such as a seasonal fruit tart, and tea, delicious hot chocolate or coffee. Ⓐ 102 Boulevard du Montparnasse Ⓣ 01 43 20 14 20 Ⓛ 08.00–01.00 Mon–Fri, 08.30–01.30 Sat & Sun Ⓝ Metro: Vavin

**Les Deux Magots & Café de Flore £** ❷ & ❸   Since the late 19th/early 20th century, these two famous cafés on boulevard Saint-Germain have welcomed writers, artists and intellectuals, including Trotsky, Hemingway, Camus, Sartre and Simone de Beauvoir. Today, both sponsor writers' prizes to keep up the literary tradition.
**Les Deux Magots** has comfy wood chairs, polished glass and brass, waiters in bow ties, black suits and long white aprons, and a view of the tower of the Saint-Germain-des-Prés church. €6.50 for a thick

and delicious *chocolat chaud* (hot chocolate). English newspapers are available. **ⓐ** 6 Place Saint-Germain-des-Prés **ⓕ** 01 45 48 55 25 **ⓛ** 07.30–01.00 **ⓝ** Metro: Saint-Germain-des-Prés

**Café de Flore** is just as charming, and the hot chocolate here, served in a Flore-engraved silver jug, equals that of the neighbouring Deux Magots. **ⓐ** 172 boulevard Saint-Germain **ⓕ** 01 45 48 55 26 **ⓛ** 07.00–01.00 **ⓝ** Metro: Saint-Germain-des-Prés

**Ecritoire £** **❹** Just steps from the Sorbonne, this is a pleasant place to stop for a break or a light meal. With its mirrored interior and street tables in fine weather, it is traditionally Parisian. It serves salads and sandwiches as well as light meals. **ⓐ** 3 Place de la Sorbonne **ⓕ** 01 43 54 60 02 **ⓛ** 07.30–midnight **ⓝ** RER B: Luxembourg

**Le Procope £** **❺** Here in the oldest café in Paris (1686), Diderot and d'Alembert began compiling their encyclopaedia in 1727. Le Procope is known for its *cuisine traditionnelle*. **ⓐ** 13 rue de l'Ancienne Comédie **ⓕ** 01 40 46 79 00 **ⓛ** until 01.00 **ⓝ** Metro: Odéon

## AFTER DARK

### Restaurants
**La Brasserie Saint Benoît £** **❻** Good traditional French fare, often with a complimentary kir, is served in this simple restaurant in the Saint-Germain district. Charges are around €13.50 for the lunch menu and €24.50 for dinner. **ⓐ** 26 rue Saint Benoît **ⓕ** 01 45 48 29 66 **ⓛ** 12.00–14.30 & 18.00–midnight, closed Sun lunch **ⓝ** Metro: Saint-Germain-des-Prés

**◐** *Quintessential Parisian café*

**Café du Commerce £** ❼ The historic café is spread over three levels around an atrium hung with cascading vines with a décor that evokes an earlier era. With starters such as excellent *salade chèvre chaud* (hot goat's cheese salad) and varied main courses such as grilled pork knuckle, steak with pepper sauce or fish of the day, the Commerce is excellent value. ⓐ 51 rue du Commerce ☎ 01 45 75 03 27 🕐 12.00–15.00 & 19.00–midnight Ⓜ Metro: Ave Émile Zola or Commerce

**Orestes £** ❽ A lively French restaurant run by Greeks, this simple establishment in the Saint-Michel district has been in business since 1922. Food is copious, but often average, yet the atmosphere is fun and prices are very low. ⓐ 4 rue de Grégoire de Tours ☎ 01 43 54 62 01 🕐 12.00–14.30 & 18.00–23.30, closed Sun Ⓜ Metro: Odéon

**Altitude 95 £–££** ❾ If prices in the Jules Verne (see opposite) are too stratospheric, the Altitude 95 (95m above sea level) is reasonably priced and has a pretty panoramic view, too. ⓐ Level One, Eiffel Tower ☎ 01 45 55 20 04 🕐 12.00–midnight Ⓜ Metro: Bir-Hakeim

**Au Gourmand £–££** ❿ This new (by Parisian standards) restaurant, across the street from the Luxembourg garden and just a block from the Musée du Luxembourg, offers elegant fare at reasonable prices. The menu includes a variety of seafood dishes and roasts, steaks and chops accompanied by excellent truffle mashed potatoes. ⓐ 22 rue de Vaugirard ☎ 01 43 26 26 45 🕐 lunch weekdays, dinner Mon–Sat night Ⓜ RER B: Luxembourg

**Le Ziryab ££** ⓫ Known for its couscous and its fabulous view of the Notre-Dame and the Seine, this Moroccan restaurant sits atop the

Institut du Monde Arabe (see 'Ethnic Paris' pages 118–20). ⓐ 1 rue Fossés-Saint-Bernard ⓣ 01 53 10 10 20 ⓛ lunch 12.00–14.30, tea salon 15.00–18.00, dinner 18.30–23.00, closed Mon ⓝ Metro: Jussieu

**Le Jules Verne £££** ⓬ For high-class, high-altitude (and high-priced) fare, try the 1-star Le Jules Verne restaurant, located on the second level of the Eiffel Tower 125 m (410 ft) above ground. The restaurant has its own elevator and terrace. Diners have an excellent view of the city stretched along the river. ⓐ Level Two, Eiffel Tower ⓣ 01 45 55 61 44 ⓛ 12.15–13.45 & 19.15–21.45 ⓝ Metro: Bir-Hakeim

### Bars, clubs & entertainment
**Bâteau Six Huit** The Seine becomes the scene at night in this dance club. ⓐ quai Montebello ⓦ www.six-huit.com ⓝ Metro: St-Michel

**Batofar** Another buzzing and popular dance club on the Seine. ⓐ 11 quai François-Mauriac ⓦ www.batofar.org ⓝ Metro: Quai de la Gare

**Caveau de la Huchette** Located in a basement cellar, this is a jazz institution in the heart of Saint-Michel. ⓐ 5 rue de la Huchette ⓣ 01 43 26 65 05 ⓛ from 21.30 ⓝ Metro: St-Michel

**Gare Montparnasse** Watch a night-time phenomenon roll through the Left Bank every Friday night, when some 15,000 proficient roller-bladers take over the streets, leaving from the Gare Montparnasse at 22.00 and gliding through Paris until 01.00. ⓦ www.pari-roller.com ⓝ Metro: Montparnasse-Bienvenüe

**La Mezzanine de l'Alcazar** The Mezzanine bar of the Alcazar restaurant is lively with DJs or pop/rock singers, creating a great

ambience for a drink or a dance. ⓐ 62 rue Mazarine ⓣ 01 53 10 19 99
ⓦ www.alcazar.fr ⓛ 19.00–02.00 ⓝ Metro: Odéon

**Le Bar du Marché** This fashionable bar on the corner of Buci and rue
de Seine is *branché* (trendy) by night and great for people-watching
on sunny afternoons as a sidewalk café. Waiters wear overalls, the
market vendors' dress code of yore. ⓐ 75 rue de Seine ⓣ 01 43 26 55
15 ⓛ 07.30–02.00 ⓝ Metro: Mabillon

### Night views
The **Musée National du Moyen Age** in the Hôtel de Cluny is
impressive enough by day, with its medieval artefacts and tapestries,
but spotlit at night (seen along boulevard Saint-Michel) this ancient
building with its Gallo-Roman baths is an awesome, impressive site
in central Paris. ⓐ 6 Place Paul-Painlevé ⓝ Metro: Cluny-La Sorbonne
　　The **Seine** and its bridges and *bâtiments* (buildings) illuminated
at night are a majestic sight, for tourists as well as Paris residents.
　　The **Tour Eiffel** naturally steals the skyline show each night, when
it is bathed in gold and sparkling on the hour, but views from the
top of the **Tour Montparnasse** are also exquisite on a clear night and
well worth the elevator ride to the top (see pages 106–7).

### MULTI-ETHNIC PARIS
Elegant African ladies in brilliantly coloured and patterned
robes and headscarves carry huge bundles on the Paris
metro. In teashops, men puff on hookahs. In a downtown
café, a man in flowing desert robes ambles up to the bar.
People from all over the world congregate in this
cosmopolitan city.

Immigrants from France's former colonies, especially West and North Africa and Indo-China, as well as those from China, the Caribbean and Eastern Europe, give Paris its international flair. This translates into intriguing galleries, shops selling goods from around the world, and a fine collection of restaurants serving foreign cuisine.

Even in the pulsing heart of the 5th *arrondissement*, the Cyber Café Latino and the Tampico restaurant give a Latin flavour to a predominantly Greek and French-budget nightlife area. In the earthy rue St Denis area in the 1st, the sign outside the Café Jip's says 'Ambience Afro-Cuban'.

Generally, though, particular ethnic groups congregate in certain city quarters, such as the predominantly North African and Black African Goutte d'Or in the 18th *arrondissement* and the Cambodian, Vietnamese, Laotian and Chinese in the 13th. The main Jewish community is based around the rue des Rosiers in the Marais, with its delicatessens and restaurants.

In the culturally diverse Belleville area in the north of the city, there are Thai and Vietnamese restaurants, Turkish cafés, Arab grocery stores and kosher butchers. Menilmontant, east of République, is a neighbourhood of couscous and *tagine* (a slow-cooked meat, fruit and vegetable dish) restaurants competing with those serving Senegalese cuisine, and of Asian supermarkets, Vietnamese diners and shops selling Tunisian artefacts.

Little India in the 10th *arrondissement* started in a covered arcade, Passage Brady. Indian and Pakistani grocers, stores selling traditional Indian saris and incense, and curry restaurants have now spread out around the neighbourhood.

The Barbès-Rochechouart metro station is an outpost of Black Africa and the West Indies, with women in dazzling, flowing dresses, food markets selling tropical produce and exotic spices and African music blasting from small souvenir shops.

Nearby, La Goutte d'Or is the North African sector, with its couscous restaurants, Muslim bakers making fresh Algerian pastries every day, and shops stocking colourful clothes.

Arab culture is officially displayed in the fine Institut du Monde Arabe (Institute of the Arab World) opened in 1987. The 1,600 exterior panels covering the south façade adjust automatically according to the amount of available sunlight to create a moody atmosphere. Besides the museum's extensive display of Arab culture, the Institut has a library, shop, Arab tea salon serving mint tea, and a rooftop terrace and restaurant with a superb view of the Seine and Notre-Dame.

Chinatown, near the Place d'Italie metro station, is as much Southeast Asian as Chinese. Giant supermarkets such as Tangs Frères sell every conceivable delicacy of the East, including galangal, fish paste, dried lemongrass, chunks of tamarind, and fresh Chinese vegetables such as bok choy, as well as tinned, frozen and dried foods. In this area, Asian clothes such as Vietnamese tops and Chinese silk dresses are sold at discount prices. Other stores sell a variety of Asian home goods and decorations, including Chinese kitchenware, plastic chopsticks, paper lanterns and wooden Buddha statues. Local restaurants serve Vietnamese pho, barbecued duck, noodles and other Asian fast food.

◗ *Medieval masterpiece: the Cathédrale Notre-Dame at Reims*

**OUT OF TOWN**
trips

# Auvers-sur-Oise

For fans of Vincent van Gogh, it is moving to visit the village of Auvers-sur-Oise. The artist lived his last two months here, painting some of his most famous works, before dying a tragic death. The artist took such solace in Auvers, which he called 'seriously beautiful, set as it is against a vast countryside that's typical and picturesque', that he painted madly and passionately, producing 78 works during his time here.

While it was nearly 150 years ago that Van Gogh lived in Auvers, some 30 km (18½ miles) northwest of Paris, this delightful village with its stone houses, pretty gardens, cobbled streets and scent of wood-burning fires is much the way it was in the artist's day.

Today, Auvers is still very much a vibrant artists' community, with a number of galleries throughout the village, even adjacent to the train station. And the masterpieces painted by Van Gogh and other famous artists in Auvers are indicated throughout the village by signs called La Mémoire des Lieux, where copies of the paintings are shown at the locations of the scenes painted.

The Auvers Tourist Office has brochures, including those of self-guided walks, with maps marking the famous attractions and settings of Van Gogh's works. The museum of the artist Daubigny is located above the tourist office. ❸ Manoir des Colombières, rue de la Sansonne ❶ 01 30 36 10 06 ❻ daily

## GETTING THERE
### By rail
Take the SNCF train from Gare du Nord or Gare St-Lazare to Pontoise, change for Auvers-sur-Oise (direction Creil). Trains are frequent with a total journey time of one hour. A Sunday service

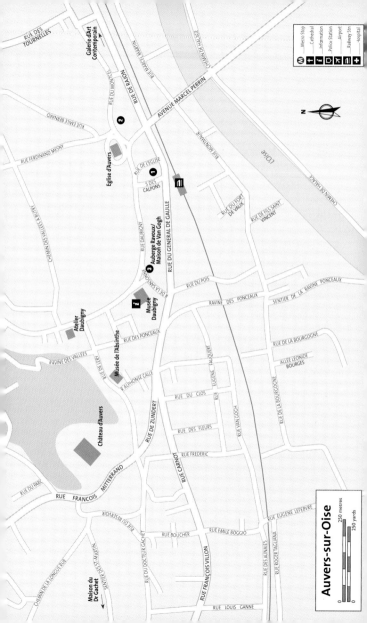

RUE DES TOURNELLES

Galerie d'Art Contemporain

RUE DU MONCEL

RUE DE BALON

RUE EMILE BERNARD

RUE FERDINAND MESNIL

CHEMIN DES VALLÉES À BITRY

RUE MARCEL MARTIN

CHEMIN DE HALAGE

AVENUE MARCEL PERRIN

❷

Église d'Auvers

RUE DE L'ÉGLISE

S DES CALPONS

RUE DU MONTMALLE

RUE DU FORT DE VAUX

RUE DU FILS SAINT VINCENT

OISE

CHEMIN DE HALAGE

RUE DAUBIGNY

Auberge Ravoux/ Maison de Van Gogh ❸

RUE DU GÉNÉRAL DE GAULLE

R DE LA SANSONNE

RUE DU POIS

RAVINE DES PONCEAUX

SENTIER DE LA RAVINE PONCEAUX

Atelier Daubigny

Musée Daubigny

RUE DE LÉRY

RUE DES PONCEAUX

RUE DE LA BOURGOGNE

Musée de l'Absinthe

RAVINE DES VALLÉES

R ALPHONSE CALLE

RUE EUGÈNE TALQUERT

ALLÉE LÉONIDE BOURGES

Château d'Auvers

RUE DU CLOS

RUE DE LA BOURGOGNE

RUE DE ZUNDERT

RUE DES FLEURS

RUE VAN GOGH

RUE DU PARC

RUE FRANCOIS MITTERRAND

RUE CARNOT

RUE FRÉDÉRIC

RUE DU RÉSERVOIR

RUE DU DOCTEUR GACHET

RUE EUGÈNE LEFEBVRE

Maison du Dr Gachet

CHEMIN DE LA LONGUE RUE

SENTIER DES ST-MARTIN

RUE BOUCHER

RUE ÉMILE BOGGIO

RUE FRANCOIS VILLON

RUE DES AUNAIES

RUE ROGER TAGLIANA

RUE LOUIS GANNE

N

Auvers-sur-Oise

0          250 metres
0          250 yards

leaves Gare du Nord at 09.29, arriving in Auvers at 09.57. Return journey is at 18.22 and an adult return costs €4.

### By road

Take the A15 in the direction of Cergy-Pontoise, leave the motorway at Exit 7 and take the RN 184 (direction Beauvais) as far as Méry-sur-Oise, then follow the signs for Auvers-sur-Oise.

## SIGHTS & ATTRACTIONS

### Château d'Auvers

An excellent introduction into the Impressionist period in Auvers is the Château d'Auvers' audio-visual romp through the world of such artists as Daubigny, Pissarro, Cézanne and Renoir. Using infrared headsets, the 'Voyages au temps des Impressionists' brings some 500 paintings to life.

ⓐ rue de Léry ⓣ 01 34 48 48 45 ⓦ www.chateau-auvers.fr
ⓛ 10.30–18.00 Mon–Fri, until 18.30 Sat & Sun (summer); 10.30–16.30 Mon–Fri, until 17.30 Sat & Sun (winter)

### L'Eglise d'Auvers

Perhaps the most poignant sight for many visitors is the church here. The delightful painting of it, *L'Eglise d'Auvers*, framed by a vibrant blue sky, now hangs in the Musée d'Orsay in Paris. The Romano-Gothic church is topped by a bell tower.

### Maison de Van Gogh

Van Gogh lived his final days in a tiny attic room in the Auberge Ravoux, also called the Maison de Van Gogh. The room, sparse and emotion-filled, with a tiny skylight, has been preserved as it was when Van Gogh died here, after shooting himself in despair. One feels the emotion and the sadness the artist felt toward the end, evident in such paintings as *Wheatfield with Crows*. Yet Van Gogh produced many cheerful and vibrant works, such as the *Escalier d'Auvers*, a delightful scene of a staircase at the top of rue de la Sansonne. Stepping outside his last abode, you can be instantly cheered by seeing this largely unchanged scene.

⏺ *The beautiful l'Eglise d'Auvers inspired Vincent Van Gogh*

Van Gogh produced many other famous and important works in Auvers, such as his self-portrait, the *Portrait of Dr Gachet*, and *Miss Gachet in her Garden*, all now hanging in the Musée d'Orsay in Paris. Van Gogh never lived to see his dream of 'having an exhibition of my own in a café'. The Van Gogh Institute is now dedicating its efforts towards bringing back one of his Auvers canvases to the room where he lived. An empty picture frame hangs on his attic room wall, awaiting that day.

ⓐ Place de la Mairie ⓣ 01 30 36 60 60 ⓛ 10.00–18.00 Mar–Oct, closed Mon & Tues

### Musée de l'Absinthe (Absinthe Museum)

A heady influence on many artists of the period, including Van Gogh, was absinthe, a potent aperitif that preceded today's aniseed drink. Called the 'Green Fairy', the cloudy green beverage could be ruinous, as many lithographs and posters depict in the excellent Musée de l'Absinthe. The writer Oscar Wilde admitted to seeing 'monstrous and cruel things' when under the influence, but was later inspired to ask, 'Is there any difference between a glass of absinthe and a sunset?'

ⓐ 44 rue Callé ⓣ 01 30 36 83 26 ⓛ 11.00–18.00 Sat, Sun & holidays (Mar–15 Dec); also 13.30–18.00 Wed, Thur & Fri (15 June–15 Sept); closed 15 Dec–beg Mar

### RETAIL THERAPY

**Auvers Tourist Office** Lots of art books and postcards, but also little art trinkets, such as painters'-palette earrings. Contact details on page 122.

**Château d'Auvers boutique** This boutique is well stocked with art books and objets d'art. Same hours and contact details as the Château (see page 124).

**Galerie d'Art Contemporain** This contemporary art gallery holds exhibitions of artists' work and sells reproductions of Van Gogh works as well as original works of contemporary amateur artists. ⓐ 5 rue Montcel ⓣ 01 34 48 00 10 ⓦ www.auversomc.com

## TAKING A BREAK

**Au Verre Placide £** ❶   A relaxing place to have a sandwich of hearty country bread, drink or light meal, its name is a play on words for the village. Meals are served in set menus or à la carte. Local artists' work adorning the walls is for sale. ⓐ 20 rue du General de Gaulle ⓣ 01 34 48 02 11 ⓛ lunch & dinner (except Wed and Sun nights), closed Mon

**Le Chemin des Peintres £** ❷   Located in an 1848 building, this charming restaurant/tea salon serves both traditional and inventive cuisine. Products from local farms and producers. ⓐ 3 bis rue de Paris ⓣ 01 30 36 14 15 ⓛ lunch 12.00–15.00 (except Wed), dinner 19.00–23.00 Sat, tea salon 10.00–12.00 & 15.00–19.00 Sat & Sun

**Auberge Ravoux £–££** ❸   An artists' café since 1876, this cosy restaurant in the Maison Van Gogh serves meals such as Van Gogh may have enjoyed. *Gigot de Sept Heures* (lamb) is a house speciality. ⓐ Place de la Mairie ⓣ 01 30 36 60 60 ⓛ lunch 12.00–16.00, tea salon 16.00–18.00, closed Mon, Tues & Nov–end Feb

# Reims

Reims, 143 km (89 miles) northeast of Paris in the heart of Champagne country, is the Mecca for lovers of the bubbly stuff. This area is noted for its tumultuous history, gentle countryside, one of Europe's finest Gothic cathedrals and, mainly, for its grape products. Set among the extensive hills of vineyards, atop some 250 km (155 miles) of chalk caves storing millions of bottles of aging effervescent wine, Reims is an attractive city well worth at least a day trip from Paris.

Europe's northernmost grape-growing area is a pleasant train ride from the French capital. The first sign of Champagne country comes just outside the town of Epernay, where the grand buildings of some venerable Champagne houses, like ornate railway stations, are seen to the right. Soon after come vineyards planted with orderly rows of grapes.

There is more to Reims than Champagne, though. The 'Coronation Capital of France' is a city of ancient abbeys and modern factories, art museums, cobbled squares and modern, red-brick subdivisions.

Day tickets for buses within Reims are €2.50 and include the airport shuttle. With these, it is easy to get around to some of the Champagne houses a few blocks from the city centre, although it is also possible to walk to some with a map from the tourist board.

**Reims Tourist Board** ⓐ 2 rue Guillaume de Machault (beside the cathedral) ① 03 26 77 45 00 Ⓦ www.reims-tourisme.com

**Comité Régional du Tourisme**

Ⓦ www.tourisme-champagne-ardenne.com

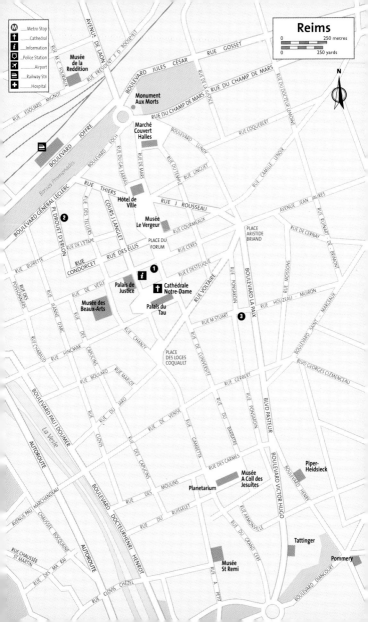

## GETTING THERE
### By rail
Trains for the one-and-three-quarter-hour trip to Reims depart from Paris several times a day from Gare de l'Est, so it is possible to leave in the morning, visit the city and several caves or vineyards, and be back in Paris by late evening. Costs vary depending on the time of day and week. For details, visit www.sncf.com

### By road
By car from Paris to Reims is 144 km (90 miles), around 1½ hours, via the A4.

## SIGHTS & ATTRACTIONS

If a pleasant stroll is what you're after, then from the train station, Place Drouet d'Erlon, a pleasant pedestrian street lined with hotels, bars, several Irish pubs and shops, leads into the city centre. A number of Roman remnants are on show right in the city, namely the Porte de Mars, enormous Roman arches dating from the year 200, and the Place du Forum, a long semi-underground Roman gallery.

### Cathédrale Notre Dame
The city centrepiece, the magnificent Notre-Dame Cathedral, is a gem of medieval architecture as impressive as the one in Paris, built in the same era.

'The outstanding handling of new architectural techniques in the 13th century, and the harmonious marriage of sculpted decoration with architecture, has made Notre-Dame in Reims one of the masterpieces of Gothic art,' says UNESCO.

● *Cathédrale Notre-Dame up close and personal*

Since Clovis in 496, France's monarchs have been crowned in this ornate cathedral, with some 2,300 statues decorating the exterior. The Gothic interior has extremely high arches and vaults with magnificent stained-glass windows at each end. At the south end, more modern windows by the painter Marc Chagall, commissioned in 1971, depict biblical scenes, using predominantly the deep blue of the stained glass used in the 15th century. The rose windows at the north end are even more impressive and ornate. The region's primary industry is even illustrated here. Some of the stained-glass windows depict the stages involved in growing grapes and making wine.

🕐 08.00–18.45 daily

**Cellar tours**

Reims was built on bubbles and its major attraction remains Champagne. The best way to appreciate it is through a tour of the cellars. More than a dozen of the famous houses offer tours, with rates averaging about €7. These are a bargain, as the price usually includes one or two glasses of Champagne, which cost about €6 each at local bars.

Guides lead tours deep into the chalk cellars, 15 to 25 m (49 to 82 feet) underground. These Roman quarries, abandoned since the 3rd century BC, were excavated to get stone for building. The subterranean labyrinths of cool caves were only later used for Champagne-making and storage. Down in the dimly-lit caverns stand row upon row of dusty Champagne bottles going through the second fermentation.

Guides explain, step by step, the complex process of producing a bottle of bubbly, from picking to fermenting to blending, the second fermentation, *remuage* (turning the bottles to collect the sediment) and *dégorgement* (removing the sediment). They impart the real sense of the pride the great houses take in producing their fine Champagnes.

In the better tours through functioning cellars, visitors might see workers suddenly arrive and start expertly turning the bottles. They may also see the *dégorgement*, the tricky process of freezing the tops of the bottles, opening them so the sediment blows out, then re-corking them.

Tours end in the tasting room, with a glass or two of the house's fine Champagne to sample. There, oenologists may explain that the effervescent beverage is best sipped from tall tulip or flute glasses, which focus the tiny, perfect bubbles in continuous streams, rather than broad, fishbowl glasses which dissipate bubbles and aroma. And the first sip may evoke Benedictine monk Dom Perignon's exclamation on tasting the first-ever Champagne in the 17th century: 'It is like drinking the stars!'

**Taittinger**, a relatively young house but with ancient cellars, provides one of the best tours. It starts with a short film in a screening room with large murals explaining the wine-making process. An extensive, one-hour tour with knowledgeable guides follows. The cellars have some ancient Abbey doors and a statue of St John the Baptist, the patron saint of cellar workers. ❸ 9 Place St-Nicaise ❶ 03 26 85 84 33 ⓦ www.taittinger.com

Nearby, the **Pommery** house is in the most impressive building, like a castle. Its traditional tour through part of its 18 km (11 miles) of cellars ends in a huge tasting room featuring an enormous carved barrel end, and massive barrels. ❸ 5 Place du Général Gourand ❶ 03 26 61 62 56 ⓦ www.pommery.com

In the **Piper-Heidsieck** (pronounced 'peeper') tours, a little automated amusement-ride car runs along tracks through the cellar with a taped announcement, all to dramatic organ music.

# GODARD

# SPÉCIALISTE
# DU FOIE GRAS

The cars pass bunches of concrete stone grapes, the size of beach balls, hanging from the walls, giant hands holding grapes, and statues of men doing the turning. It is more like a theme park than an authentic Champagne cellar. ⓐ 51 boulevard Henry Vasnier ⓣ 03 26 84 43 44 ⓦ www.piper-heidsieck.com

Details on all Champagne houses are to be found at www.umc.fr. The tourist office has all the information on Champagne tours and the addresses of the cellars. Some tours are by appointment only or for groups. Others have regular tours and it is just a matter of showing up.

**Vineyard tours**

Outside of the cellars, there are above-ground tours of the earlier part of the process – the growing and harvesting of grapes from Reims. Minibuses follow the official Route du Champagne tourist trail through the vineyards and past ancient villages. Some go to the quaint village of Hautvillers, and the old abbey of Hautvillers where Dom Perignon lived and discovered how to put the fizz into the wine. Part of the abbey, greatly damaged during the French Revolution, is now a Champagne museum. Various tableaux depict how the innovative monk first stopped the bottles with cork (an idea from Spanish monks) and how he gave them their distinctive, long-necked shape.

A typical vineyard tour for groups of two to eight people, in a minibus, is €20 per person. They depart from Epernay Tourist Office at 09.30 and 14.30 according to the season.
ⓐ 11 rue du Bas, 51530 Mancy ⓣ 03 26 59 45 85
ⓦ www.champagne-domimoreau.com

◐ *Local produce in Reims*

**Hot-air ballooning**

If you want to get really high on the Champagne region, take a hot-air balloon ride. Inflated balloons carrying four or five passengers lift gently away, over the slopes, where grapes grow in patterned fields, the rows as orderly as bottles in the long cellars. The trip ends, appropriately enough, with ground crew waiting with fluted glasses, silver ice buckets and bottles of chilled *grand cru*. The local tourist office has information on hot-air balloon flights, which cost about €100 a person.

## RETAIL THERAPY

Souvenir shops in the tourist information office and local stores sell boxes of St Rémi Galettes (cookies; €2.50 a box of 12); sandstone gargoyle replicas of the ones on the cathedral for €37 and other sandstone carvings of vineyard workers for about €55. All the Champagne houses have shops selling their products.

**Caves des Sacrés** On the square facing the cathedral, this place has a wide range of souvenirs, from postcards and fridge magnets to fine, locally-made tapestries. Works 68 x 125 cm (27 x 49 inches) cost €265, while larger ones, 138 x 228 cm (54 x 90 inches) are €895. Champagne paraphernalia, such as elegant glass flutes with holders for €18.90 to €33 for a set of six, and silver-plated ice buckets for €39.90, are popular. Local products offered include jars of mustard for €2 or €3, local vinegars at €4 per bottle, and Champagne-cork-shaped chocolates with Marc de Champagne liqueurs inside them for €5 per 14. ❸ 5 Place du Cardinal Luçon

▶ *La Boutique Champenoise*

**La Boutique Champenoise** Next door to the Caves des Sacrés, this wine store has 500 different types of Champagne, an impressive collection. The cheapest is €12.90; the most expensive is around €500.

## TAKING A BREAK

**Café du Palais £ ❶** While this atmospheric café may be popular with tourists, by far the greatest number of clientele is local. Very good, friendly service accompanies the excellent wine list and fine family food (mum cooks the main courses, daughter the sweets, and the son manages the front). Lunch only, as the café closes at 20.30.
🍴 14 Place Myron-Herrich ☎ 03 26 47 52 54

**Le Grand Café £ ❷** With its wood and mirrors, paintings and old black-and-white photographs of France, this café is a visual treat. The speciality of the house is *moules frites* (mussels with chips) and Champagne. 🍴 92 Place Drouet d'Erlon ☎ 03 26 79 19 89

**Le Vigneron £ ❸** The wine-maker restaurant is like a wine museum with thematic wall posters, wicker grape baskets, ploughs, wine kegs, line drawings and cartoons of Champagne subjects. All this with fine food and service. Try the local aperitif Ratafia (fortified red wine with oranges).
🍴 Place Paul Jamot ☎ 03 26 79 86 70

❍ *Follow the signs*

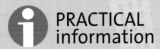

Musée du
Luxembourg

Jeux - Attractions
Rucher

Poste des
surveillants

## Directory

### GETTING THERE

**By air**

Eight major airlines now fly to France from 14 gateways. New budget airlines now connect several secondary UK destinations to the French capital. The two major international airports in Paris are Roissy-Charles de Gaulle (handling most international flights) and Orly (most domestic and some European routes), while Beauvais specialises in charter flights.

**Orly (ORY)** ℹ (06.00–23.45) 08 92 68 15 15 (€0.34/min) ⓦ www.adp.fr

**Paris-Beauvais (BVA)** ℹ (08.00–22.30) 08 92 68 20 66 or 08 92 68 20 73 (€0.37/min) ⓦ www.aeroportbeauvais.com

**Roissy-Charles de Gaulle (CDG)** ℹ 08 92 68 15 15 (€0.34/min) ⓦ www.adp.fr

**Air Canada** ℹ 08 25 88 08 81
**Air France** ℹ 08 20 82 08 20
**American Airlines** ℹ 08 10 87 28 72
**British Airways** ℹ 08 25 82 54 00
**Delta Airlines** ℹ 08 11 64 00 05
**easyJet** ℹ 08 25 08 25 08
**KLM/Northwest Airlines** ℹ 08 90 71 07 10
**RyanAir** ℹ 08 92 68 20 73
**United** ℹ 08 10 72 72 72
**US Airways** ℹ 08 10 63 22 22
**Virgin** ℹ 08 21 23 02 02

Many people are aware that air travel emits $CO_2$, which contributes to climate change. You may be interested in the possibility of

lessening the environmental impact of your flight through the
charity Climate Care, which offsets your $CO_2$ by funding
environmental projects around the world. Visit www.climatecare.org

**By rail**

The Eurostar provides fast, seamless connections from London's
Waterloo station to central Paris (Gare du Nord) in two-and-a-half to
three hours. By booking two months or more in advance, you can
get great savings. Travel mid-week is cheaper than on weekends.
ⓦ www.eurostar.com

The Thalys high-speed train links Paris to Brussels and
Amsterdam. ⓦ www.thalys.com

For information and tickets for all rail travel (including high-
speed trains called TGV) in France and Europe, contact the SNCF
or visit one of their offices in Paris. ⓘ 08 92 35 35 35, or just 36 35
(in French) ⓦ www.sncf.fr

ⓘ Before travelling on any train in France, you must *composter*
(punch or validate) your ticket in one of the machines located at
platform entrances.

⬤ *Travel in style*

## By road
### Car

Travelling by car from Calais to Paris, the 289 km (179 miles) takes just under three hours. Take the N1 south. Depending on where you approach Paris from, you'll join the ring road at one of the 30 *portes* (gateways) that punctuate the 35 km (21 miles) of expressway. Based on the area you are heading towards, you have a choice between the *périphérique intérieur* (inner ring road), which runs in a clockwise direction, and the *périphérique extérieur* (outer ring road), which runs counter-clockwise.

Traffic flow and journey times between gateways are displayed on illuminated overhead panels. Exit signs for each gateway into the city are given plenty of time in advance, so you can make sure you get in the right-hand lane. The speed limit is 80 km/h (50 mph) on ring roads and 50 km/h (30 mph) in urban areas. Be on the lookout for speed checks.

🛈 Driving is on the right and seat belts are mandatory.

## Bus

Coaches depart every two days from May to the end of October, leaving from London. A one-way ticket costs £25.
Ⓦ www.busabout.com

## By sea

There are many connections from Britain to France by sea. For information on the main ferry services, see www.directferries.co.uk, www.condorferries.co.uk, www.aferry.co.uk and www.brittany-ferries.co.uk

## ENTRY FORMALITIES

Citizens of EU countries need only a current valid identity card to enter France, but should bring their passports as well. Citizens of Australia, Canada, Finland, New Zealand, Norway, Sweden and the US need a passport but not a visa to enter France, and can stay for up to 90 days. South Africans need a tourist visa. Contact the Consulat Général de France in Johannesburg (ⓐ PO Box 1027 Parklands 2101) or Visa Services (ⓐ 191 Jan Smuts Ave, 3rd floor, Standard Bank Building, Rosebank 2196 ⓣ (27) 11 778 56 00 ⓦ www.consulfrance-jhb.org). All other passport holders should check with the nearest French embassy or consulate. For more information, see www.diplomatie.gouv.fr

Visitors may bring in personal possessions and goods for personal use. The Single European Market allows visitors to bring in and take out most things as long as taxes have been paid on them in an EU country and they are for personal consumption. For more information, contact www.douane.gouv.fr

## MONEY

The euro is the currency of France and many other countries in the EU. €1 is divided into 100 cents. Notes come in €5, €10, €20, €50, €100, €200 and €500. Coins come in €1 and €2 and in 1, 2, 5, 10, 20 and 50 cents.

*Bureaux de change* (currency exchange outlets), available at train stations, airports and main bank branches, are usually open late. Check buying/selling exchange rates and commission charged by agencies before using their service. If you have an international credit or cash card, automatic teller machines (ATMs) are widely available and most have service in English. By far the majority of travellers today use ATMs, the most economical system. Credit cards are widely accepted, particularly Visa and Mastercard.

The following numbers are useful if you lose your credit cards:

**American Express** ⓘ 01 47 77 72 00
**Carte Bleue/Visa** ⓘ 08 92 705 705
**Diner's Club** ⓘ 08 10 31 41 59
**Eurocard/Mastercard** ⓘ 01 45 67 84 84
**JCB** ⓘ 01 42 86 06 01

### HEALTH, SAFETY & CRIME

There are no special food and drink precautions. Tap water is potable, unless otherwise marked. France is famous for its excellent health care, and the European Health Insurance Card entitles citizens from EU countries to the state-funded health care scheme in France or other EU countries in which they are staying. (For more information in Britain, see www.direct.gov.uk.) For non-EU travellers, however, it can be expensive, so you should purchase your own health insurance before travelling.

In an emergency, call SAMU (dial 15), the emergency ambulance service. Aspirin and other basic medicines are available at pharmacies (indicated with a green cross), many of which are open on Sundays.

### Streetwise safety precautions

Violent crime is rare in the main city and around the major tourist sights, although some of the *banlieues* (suburbs) are not safe after dark. However, pickpocketing is widespread, especially on the metro and other public transport, at major tourist sights and even in museums, so keep your bags and wallets closed and well out of reach, and be vigilant. Backpacks, particularly their front-zippered pockets, are a new target for pickpockets, so don't keep anything valuable in those, unless you carry them in front of you.

Valuables, including important documents, should be left in your hotel safe if possible. Avoid carrying large cameras and purses and other things that will make you a tourist target.

Pedestrians should be extremely careful when crossing the road; watch out for cars, motorbikes, scooters and even roller-bladers, as the average Parisian tends to take liberties where road safety is concerned. Look both ways before crossing, and make sure you respect the zebra crossings and traffic lights, as some drivers won't. Parisians of all ages seem to enjoy the thrill of dashing across at the last second. Don't attempt to do the same.

Hostess bars, particularly in the Pigalle neighbourhood, can charge exorbitant prices, so beware.

If you do require assistance, police are fairly obvious in dark-blue uniforms with the word 'police' prominently displayed. They are quite helpful, although most do not speak much English.

## OPENING HOURS

Most services, shops and businesses are open all day from 09.00 or 09.30 to 18.00 or 19.00. Major department stores usually stay open late one night per week. Smaller boutiques often open later in the mornings, at around 10.00 or 11.00. On Sunday, most shops and businesses are closed, although Sunday shopping is prevalent in the Marais district and around the quays of Canal St-Martin.

Banking hours are usually 09.00–16.30 on weekdays, though some banks are open on Saturday.

Most museums are closed either Monday or Tuesday, but the larger ones have at least one night per week when they'll stay open until around 22.00.

## TOILETS

Some public toilets, which are usually quite clean, can be found in Paris. They are supervised and cost around €0.40, closing in the evenings. Coin-operated 'superloos' are available also at €0.40 and are automatically cleaned after each visitor. While cafés do not usually welcome people using their toilets unless they are paying customers, some don't mind and have coin entry (usually €0.20). Some toilets here are unisex. Department stores offer free toilet facilities. Shopping centres and arcades also usually have toilets,

▲ *There's lots for the children to do, too*

some free, some not. You have to pay to go to the toilets in railway stations, but they are free at the airports. You will also find supervised toilets in most of the large parks and gardens in the city.

## CHILDREN

Paris is reasonably child-friendly, and children are welcome in restaurants (although not as much as dogs). Getting around by metro can be tiring for young children, however, as there are a lot of climbs and long walks in the stations. This can also be hard for parents trying to manipulate strollers. Baby food and nappies are available in supermarkets throughout the city.

Attractions and activities especially suitable for children can be found at www.parisinfo.com, and include the following:

- **Bois de Vincennes** The Ferme de Paris is a farm in the east side of this area, featuring farm animals and a vegetable garden tended by children. From 31 May to 13 Sept, kids can enjoy 'Pestacles' (music festival for children) in the wood's Parc Floral.
  **La Ferme de Paris** ✉ route de Pesage, Bois de Vincennes ☎ 01 43 28 47 63 🕐 13.30–19.00, closed Mon (summer); 13.30–17.00 Sat & Sun (winter) Ⓜ Metro: Chateâu-de-Vincennes

- **Cité des Enfants** This attraction at La Villette (northeast) is full of interactive learning activities for youngsters aged 3 to 12. For contact details, see Cité des Sciences (page 87).

- **Disneyland Resort Paris** This is probably the biggest attraction for most kids, and is accessible by RER A east to Marne-la-Vallée-Chessy. ☎ 01 60 30 60 53 🌐 www.disneylandparis.com 🕐 10.00–20.00 Mon–Fri, 09.00–20.00 Sat & Sun

- **Jardin d'Acclimatation** This park in the Bois de Boulogne (west side) includes an old-fashioned puppet theatre, miniature train, merry-go-round and Exploradôme, with arts and science exhibits. ⓐ Bois de Boulogne ① 01 40 67 90 82 ① 10.00–18.00 Ⓝ Metro: Sablons

- **Jardin du Luxembourg** With its small boat rentals and ornamental pond, puppet theatre and pony rides, this garden is always a good choice. ⓐ rue de Vaugirard ① sunrise–sunset Ⓝ RER B: Luxembourg

- **Palais de la Découverte (Palace of Discovery)** Kids can enjoy interactive exhibits here, including those in astronomy and earth sciences. ⓐ avenue Franklin Roosevelt ① 01 56 43 20 21 ⓦ www.palais-decouverte.fr ① 09.30–18.00 Tues–Sat, 10.00–19.00 Sun Ⓝ Metro: Champs-Elysées Clémenceau

## COMMUNICATIONS
### Public telephones
*Télécartes* (telephone cards) in two sizes (50 units for €6 and 120 units for €15) are on sale at *tabacs* (tobacco stores), newsstands and main metro and RER stations. Public phones are found in post offices, railway and metro stations and in the street, and in some bars and restaurants. They generally take telephone cards and credit cards.

### Mobile phones
As in the rest of Europe, all GSM-compatible phones should be useable in France. You can get a French telephone number at any telecom shop if you want to avoid being charged international rates

but want to retain your current operator. Otherwise you can sign up with one of the French operators – Orange, SFR or Bouyges Télécom – but be aware that they will often try to lock you into long-term contracts. You can also rent cellphones, a good choice being Cellhire (ⓐ 182 avenue Charles de Gaulle, 92522 Neuilly sur Seine ☎ 01 41 43 79 40 🌐 www.cellhire.fr).

## TELEPHONING FRANCE
To telephone France from abroad, dial the international code first (usually 00), then 33 and the number (skipping the first '0'). All numbers in France have ten digits and start with 0. In Paris, they start with 01.

## TELEPHONING FROM FRANCE
To make an international call from France, dial 00 first, then the country code, followed by the local area code and the number.
Country codes:
**Australia** 61
**Canada** 1
**New Zealand** 64
**Republic of Ireland** 353
**South Africa** 27
**UK** 44
**USA** 1

**International operator** 32 12
**French directory** 12

## Post

The French postal service is reliable and efficient. The main post office, located at 52 rue du Louvre, is open 24 hours a day, though service is limited after 19.00. For *poste restante* service, letters should be addressed (preferably with the surname underlined and in capitals) to Poste Restante, 52 rue du Louvre, 75001 Paris (❶ 01 40 28 76 00). Other post offices are open 08.00–19.00 Monday to Friday and 08.00–12.00 on Saturday.

Stamps are for sale in self-serve machines in the post offices as well as *tabacs* (tobacco stores). Postboxes are yellow. Stamps for letters and cards up to 20 grams cost €0.55 within Europe and €0.90 to North America, Australia and New Zealand.

## Internet access

There is free internet access in all the main train stations, and cyber cafés are plentiful, especially in the main areas. Most cafés have a large @ in the name. However, the keyboard is generally not QWERTY, which can make using it difficult. Staff, however, are usually helpful and speak some English. XS Arena has several locations throughout Paris.

**XS Arena** ❸ 110 boulevard Saint-Germain & 31 boulevard Sebastopol ❶ 01 46 33 40 01 & 01 40 13 06 51 ❿ www.xsarena.com ❺ 24 hours

## ELECTRICITY

Electricity is 220 volts, 50 Hz, with round-pin wall sockets. UK or non-EU visitors bringing in appliances will need an adaptor, and North Americans will need a transformer as well.

## TRAVELLERS WITH DISABILITIES

Paris is making a concerted effort to assist those with disabilities. The 'Tourisme & Handicap' label on cultural and leisure sights shows access and facilities for one or more categories of disability. Some restaurants and hotels are also posting the same label. For more information see the Paris Visitors Bureau website at www.paris.info.com

A number of buses accommodate wheelchairs, and the RER A and the metro line 14 have lifts for those with limited mobility. The rest of the metro system is not yet wheelchair-friendly. The RATP (municipal transport system) issues transport network maps that show the bus routes that accommodate wheelchairs. The RER also has special ramps that can be fitted at doorways for wheelchairs. For more information, contact www.infomobi.com or call 08 10 64 64 64.

The Compagnons du Voyage, a private association, provides travel companions and works with the RATP/SNCF to enable handicapped travellers to be accompanied on the metro, RER, bus and trains. This service costs €25 per hour in the Parisian area Monday to Saturday and €37.50 on Sundays and public holidays. ☎ 01 53 11 11 12 🖷 01 53 11 11 13

For blind people or the visually impaired, the AVH (Association Valentine Haüy) is a good contact. ➌ 5 rue Duroc ☎ 01 44 49 27 27 🖷 01 44 49 27 10 🌐 www.avh.asso.fr ⊜ avh@avh.asso.fr

For information on transport in special vehicles for wheelchairs, contact the following companies and associations:

**AIHROP** Prices vary, depending on the length of voyage. ☎ 01 41 29 01 29 🖷 01 41 29 01 27

**ASA** The charge is €20 for a one-way trip, plus €5 for the accompanying personnel. ☎ 01 42 03 61 67

## FURTHER INFORMATION

**Paris Convention and Visitors Bureau, Main Welcome Centre**

ⓐ 25 rue des Pyramides ⓣ 08 92 68 30 00 (€0.34/min)
ⓦ www.parisinfo.com ⓛ 10.00–19.00 Mon–Sat, 11.00–19.00 Sun &
holidays ⓜ Metro: Pyramides

Other welcome centres, with the same telephone number and
website, are to be found throughout Paris at the following
addresses:

**Anvers Welcome Centre** ⓐ facing 72 boulevard Rochechouart
ⓛ 10.00–18.00 (except 25 Dec, 1 Jan & 1 May) ⓜ Metro: Anvers

**Carrousel du Louvre Welcome Centre** ⓐ Place de la Pyramide
Inversée, 99 rue de Rivoli ⓛ 10.00–18.00 ⓜ Metro: Palais Royal-
Musée du Louvre

**Expo/Porte de Versailles Welcome Centre** ⓐ 1 Place de la Porte de
Versailles ⓛ 11.00–19.00 during trade fairs ⓜ Metro: Porte de
Versailles

**Gare de Lyon Welcome Centre** ⓐ 20 boulevard Diderot
ⓛ 09.00–18.00 Mon–Sat (except 1 May) ⓜ Metro: Gare de Lyon

**Gare du Nord Welcome Centre** ⓐ 18 rue de Dunkerque
ⓛ 08.00–18.00 (except 25 Dec & 1 May) ⓜ Metro: Gare du Nord

**Montmartre Welcome Centre** ⓐ 21 Place du Tertre ⓛ 10.00–19.00
ⓜ Metro: Abbesses

**Opéra – Grands Magasins Welcome Centre** ⓐ 11 rue Scribe
ⓛ 09.00–18.00 Mon–Sat (except 1 May) ⓜ Metro: Opéra

**Tour Eiffel Welcome Centre** ⓐ Tour Eiffel ⓛ 11.00–18.40
25 Mar–31 Oct (except 1 May) ⓜ Metro: Bir-Hakeim

## BACKGROUND READING

Paris is one of the world's most written-about cities. Life in Paris before World War II inspired such classic memoirs as Henry Miller's *Tropic of Cancer*, Ernest Hemingway's *A Movable Feast* and Morley Callaghan's *That Summer in Paris*. Although dated, they still make good reading.

Mavis Gallant's short stories, *Overhead in a Balloon* and *Paris Stories*, are more contemporary works set in the city. On a lighter note, a series of contemporary murder mysteries by Cara Black such as *Murder in Belleville* and *Murder in the Marais*, evoke the ambience of Paris in the early 1990s. And, of course, the Dan Brown blockbuster *The Da Vinci Code* starts in Paris, before crossing the channel.

Numerous contemporary works have been written about French customs, culture and habits, and *la difference*. Many of these books are patronising efforts at 'understanding the French'. Some of the better ones include *Sixty Million Frenchmen Can't be Wrong* by Jean-Benoît Nadeau and Julie Barlow, *And God Created the French* by Louis-Bernard Robitaille, and *French or Foe* by Polly Platt. *Around and About Paris* by Thirza Vallois, in three volumes, provides an excellent walking guide, detailing Paris's history and geography.

## Useful phrases

Although English is widely spoken in Paris, these words and phrases
may come in handy. See also the phrases for specific situations in
other parts of the book.

| English | French | Approx. pronunciation |
|---|---|---|
| **BASICS** | | |
| Yes | Oui | Wee |
| No | Non | Nawng |
| Please | S'il vous plaît | Seel voo pleh |
| Thank you | Merci | Mehrsee |
| Hello | Bonjour | Bawngzhoor |
| Goodbye | Au revoir | Aw revwahr |
| Excuse me | Excusez-moi | Ekskeweh mwah |
| Sorry | Désolé(e) | Dehzoleh |
| That's okay | Ça va | Sahr vahr |
| To | À | Ah |
| From | De | Der |
| I don't speak French | Je ne parle pas français | Zher ner pahrl pah frahngsay |
| Do you speak English? | Vous parlez anglais? | Voopahrlay ahnglay? |
| Good morning | Bonjour | Bawng-zhoor |
| Good afternoon | Bonjour | Bawng-zhoor |
| Good evening | Bonsoir | Bawng-swah |
| Goodnight | Bonne nuit | Bun nwee |
| My name is ... | Je m'appelle ... | Zher mahpehl ... |
| **DAYS & TIMES** | | |
| Monday | Lundi | Langdee |
| Tuesday | Mardi | Mahrdee |
| Wednesday | Mercredi | Mehrkrerdee |
| Thursday | Jeudi | Zhurdee |
| Friday | Vendredi | Vahndrerdee |
| Saturday | Samedi | Sahmdee |
| Sunday | Dimanche | Deemahngsh |
| Morning | Le matin | Ler mahtang |
| Afternoon | L'après-midi | Lahpreh meedee |
| Evening | Le soir | Ler swahr |
| Night | La nuit | Lah nwee |
| Yesterday | Hier | Yehr |

| English | French | Approx. pronunciation |
|---|---|---|
| Today | Aujourd'hui | Ojoordewee |
| Tomorrow | Demain | Dermang |
| What time is it? | Quelle heure est-il? | Kel urr ehteel? |
| It is ... | Il est ... | Eel eh ... |
| 09.00 | Neuf heures | Nurv urr |
| Midday | Midi | Meedee |
| Midnight | Minuit | Meenurhee |

## NUMBERS

| One | Un/Une | Ang/Ewn |
|---|---|---|
| Two | Deux | Dur |
| Three | Trois | Trwah |
| Four | Quatre | Kahtr |
| Five | Cinq | Sangk |
| Six | Six | Seess |
| Seven | Sept | Seht |
| Eight | Huit | Weet |
| Nine | Neuf | Nurf |
| Ten | Dix | Deess |
| Eleven | Onze | Awngz |
| Twelve | Douze | Dooz |
| Twenty | Vingt | Vang |
| Fifty | Cinquante | Sangkahnt |
| One hundred | Cent | Sahng |

## MONEY

| I would like to change these traveller's cheques/this currency | J'aimerais changer ces chèques de voyage/ces devises | Zhaymray shahngzheh seh shek der vwahahzh/seh derveez |
|---|---|---|
| Where is the nearest ATM? | Où se trouve le distributeur de billets le plus proche? | Oo ser troov ler distribewter der beeyeh ler plew prosh? |
| Do you accept credit cards? | Vous acceptez les cartes de crédit? | Voos aksepteh leh kart der krehdee? |

## SIGNS & NOTICES

| Airport | Aéroport | Ahehrohpohr |
|---|---|---|
| Rail station/Platform | Gare/Quai | Gahr/Kay |
| Smoking/non-smoking | Fumeurs/non fumeurs | Fewmurh/nawng fewmurh |
| Toilets | Toilettes | Twahlayt |
| Ladies/Gentlemen | Femmes/Hommes | Fam/Ommh |
| Subway | Métro | Maytroa |

# Emergencies

**English-speaking health services**
The clinic of the American Hospital of Paris provides a medical and surgical emergency service 24 hours a day, 7 days a week. Patients are looked after by a bilingual team (French-English) who have access to specialists on call, covering more than 20 medical and surgical fields. There is always a cardiologist and intensive care doctor on duty. The British Hospital specializes in gynecological emergencies.

**The American Hospital in Paris** ✆ 63 boulevard Victor Hugo, Neuilly-sur-Seine ☎ 01 46 41 25 25 Ⓜ Metro: Anatole France or Pont de Levallois

**The Hertford British Hospital** ✆ 3 rue Barbès Levallois-Perret ☎ 01 46 39 22 22 Ⓜ Metro: Anatole France

**24-hour pharmacy** ✆ Les Champs, 84 avenue des Champs-Elysées ☎ 01 45 62 02 41

**EMERGENCY NUMBERS**
**Emergency services** (not for car break-downs) 112 (use from any mobile phone)
**Fire service** 18
**Police** 17
**SAMU (ambulance service)** 15
**SOS Médécins (doctors)** 01 47 07 77 77
**SOS Dentaire (dentists)** 01 43 37 51 00
**Children's burns** 01 44 73 62 54
**Adults' burns** 01 42 34 17 58
**Poison Treatment Centre** 01 40 05 48 48
**Sexually transmitted diseases (Bichat Hospital)** 01 40 78 26 00

### Police

In case of attack or theft, report it to either the nearest police station or *gendarmerie* to where the attack was carried out.

**Prefecture de police** 🏠 9 boulevard du Palais ☎ 01 53 71 53 71
🌐 www.prefecture-police-paris.interieur.gouv.fr Ⓜ Metro: Cité
**Lost and found office**, Préfecture de police 🏠 36 rue des Morillons
☎ 08 21 00 25 25 Ⓜ Metro: Convention

### Embassies & consulates

**Australia** 🏠 4 rue Jean Rey ☎ 01 40 59 33 00 Ⓜ Metro: Bir Hakeim
**Canada** 🏠 35 avenue Montaigne ☎ 01 44 43 29 00 Ⓜ Metro: Alma Marceau or F D Roosevelt
**New Zealand** 🏠 7 ter rue Léonard de Vinci ☎ 01 45 01 43 43 Ⓜ Metro: Victor Hugo
**Republic of Ireland** 🏠 4 rue Rude ☎ 01 44 17 67 00 Ⓜ Metro: Charles de Gaulle-Etoile or Argentine
**South Africa** 🏠 59 quai d'Orsay ☎ 01 53 59 23 23 Ⓜ Metro: Invalides
**UK** 🏠 35 rue du Faubourg Saint-Honoré ☎ 01 44 51 31 02 Ⓜ Metro: Madeleine or St-Lazare
**US** 🏠 2 rue Saint-Florentin ☎ 01 43 12 22 22 Ⓜ Metro: Champs-Elysées Clémenceau

### EMERGENCY PHRASES

**Help!** Au secours! *Ossercoor!*  **Fire!** Au feu! *Oh fur!*
**Stop!** Stop! *Stop!*
**Call an ambulance/a doctor/the police/the fire service!**
Appelez une ambulance/un médecin/la police/les pompiers!
*Ahperleh ewn ahngbewlahngss/ang medesang/lah poleess/leh pompeeyeh!*

**A**

accommodation 34–39
air travel 140–141
airports 48–49, 140
Arc de Triomphe 62, 64
Arènes de Lutèce 102
arts *see* culture
Auvers-sur-Oise 122–126

**B**

bars & clubs 28–29, 31,
    79, 94–95, 96–97,
    117–118
Bastille 12, 13, 80
Bastille Day 12–13
Boulevard Saint-Germain
    98
bus travel 48–49, 56–57,
    142

**C**

cafés 47, 76, 113–115, 127,
    138, 150
canal cruises 82–83
Canal St-Martin 83
car hire 58
Cathédrale Notre-Dame
    (Reims) 130–132
cellar tours (Reims)
    132–133, 135
Centre Pompidou
    18, 87
Champagne 128, 132–133,
    135–137
Champs-Elysées 64
Chapelle de la Sorbonne
    44
Château d'Auvers 124
children 147–148
Cimetière de Père-
    Lachaise 83–84
cinema 58–60, 88
Cité des Sciences 87
Conciergerie 64
consulates 157
crime 52–53, 144–145

culture 18–20, 31, 44, 46,
    58–60, 67–69, 70–73,
    86, 87–90, 107–112, 126
customs & duty 143

**D**

disabilities, travellers
    with 151
driving 52, 142

**E**

Eglise Saint-Sulpice 98
electricity 150
embassies 157
emergencies 144, 156–157
entertainment 28–31
    *see also* nightlife
events 8–13

**F**

fashion 22, 73–75, 90–91,
    113
festivals 9, 10, 11–13
Fondation Cartier 107
food & drink 24–27, 112,
    128, 132–137

**G**

Galeries Nationales du
    Grand Palais 70–71

**H**

Haussmann, Baron
    Georges Eugène 15, 62
health 144, 156
history 14–15
Hôtel des Invalides
    100
hotels 34–39
Hugo, Victor 84

**I**

Île Saint-Louis 84
internet cafés 150

**J**

Jardin des Plantes 100
Jardin des Tuileries
    64–66

Jardin du Luxembourg
    44, 100, 102

**L**

La Cinémathèque
    Française 88
language 23, 27, 56,
    154–155, 157
Latin Quarter 102
Left Bank 98
L'Eglise d'Auvers 124
lifestyle 16–17

**M**

Maison de Van Gogh
    124–126
Maison de Victor Hugo
    84
Maison Européenne de
    la Photographie 88
Marais 18, 22, 80, 85
Marché Bastille 13
markets 13, 103
Metro 53, 56–57
minivans 49
money 143–144
Montmartre 66–67
multiculturalism
    118–120
Musée Dapper 71
Musée d'Art Moderne de
    la Ville de Paris 71
Musée de la Musique
    88–89
Musée de l'Absinthe 126
Musée Delacroix 107
Musée des Arts et
    Métiers 90
Musée des Egouts 108
Musée d'Histoire
    Naturelle 108
Musée d'Orsay 108, 110
Musée du Louvre 18,
    67–69
Musée du Luxembourg
    110

Musée du Montparnasse 110
Musée du Quai Branly 18, 110–111
Musée du Vieux Montmartre 71
Musée Maillol Fondation Dina Vierny 111
Musée Marmottan Monet 71–72
Musée National des Arts Asiatiques (Guimet) 72
Musée Picasso 90
Musée Rodin 111
Musée Zadkine 111–112
music 20, 28–29, 79, 86, 96–97, 117–118

**N**
nightlife 28–31, 77–79, 94–97, 115–118
Notre-Dame (Paris) 85–86

**O**
Odéon 103
opening hours 145
opera 20, 86
Opéra Bastille 12, 20, 86

**P**
Palais Garnier: Opéra National de Paris 20, 72
Panthéon 104–105
Panthéon Bouddhique 72
Parc de la Villette 86
Paris Plage 10

passports & visas 143
Petit Palais 73
phones 148–149
Place de la Bastille 80
Place de la Concorde 69
Place de la République 87
Place de l'Hôtel de Ville 17
Place des Vosges 44
Place du Tertre 66–67
police 145, 157
post 150
public holidays 11
public transport 48–49, 53–57, 58, 122, 124, 130, 141, 142, 151

**R**
rail travel 48, 49, 56–57, 58, 122, 124, 130, 141
Reims 128–136
restaurants 24–25, 26–27, 28, 47, 77–78, 94–96, 115–117
Right Bank East 80
Right Bank West 62
river cruises 106
Rivoli 47
Rodin, Auguste 111
roller-blading 32–33, 117

**S**
Sacré-Coeur 66
safety 52–53, 144–145

Saint-Germain-des-Prés 105
Sainte-Chapelle 69
sea travel 142
seasons 8
Seine 105–106
shopping 13, 22–23, 47, 73–76, 90–93, 103, 112–113, 126–127, 136–137
sport 32–33, 70
Statues of Liberty 102

**T**
taxis 49, 57
Tenniseum 70
time differences 48
toilets 146
Tour Eiffel 18, 106
Tour Montparnasse 106–107
tourist information 152
Trocadéro 70

**V**
Van Gogh, Vincent 122, 124–126
Viaduc des Arts 12, 93
vineyard tours (Reims) 135–136

**W**
weather 8, 46–47

**Y**
youth hostels 39

The publishers would like to thank the following for supplying
the copyright photographs for this book: Garry Marchant, Pictures
Colour Library: pages 5, 7, 13, 16, 68, 109 and Christopher Holt:
page 42.

Copy editor: Anne McGregor
Proofreader: Emma Sangster

## Send your thoughts to
# books@thomascook.com

- Found a great bar, club, shop or must-see sight that we don't feature?
- Like to tip us off about any information that needs updating?
- Want to tell us what you love about this handy little guidebook and more importantly how we can make it even handier?

Then here's your chance to tell all! Send us ideas, discoveries and recommendations today and then look out for your valuable input in the next edition of this title. As an extra 'thank you' from Thomas Cook Publishing, you'll be automatically entered into our exciting monthly prize draw.

Send an email to the above address (stating the book's title) or write to: CitySpots Project Editor, Thomas Cook Publishing, PO Box 227, The Thomas Cook Business Park, Unit 18, Coningsby Road, Peterborough PE3 8SB, UK.